SEMIOTICS AND INTERPRETATION

SEMIOTICS AND INTERPRETATION

ROBERT SCHOLES

NEW HAVEN AND LONDON
YALE UNIVERSITY PRESS

Designed by Nancy Ovedovitz and set in VIP Times Roman type.
Printed in the United States of America by The Vail-Ballou Press, Binghamton, N.Y.

Acknowledgment is made to those mentioned below for permission to reprint:
Atheneum Publishers, for the poem from W. S. Merwin, "Separation" in *The Moving Target*. Copyright © 1963 by W. S. Merwin (New York: Atheneum, 1963).
Atheneum Publishers, for the poem from W. S. Merwin, "When the War is Over" in *The Lice*. Copyright © 1967 by W. S. Merwin (New York: Atheneum, 1967).
Atheneum Publishers, for the poem from W. S. Merwin, "Elegy" in *The Carrier of Ladders*. Copyright © 1970 by W. S. Merwin (New York: Atheneum, 1970).
New Directions Publishing Corporation, for "Nantucket" in *Collected Earlier Poems* by William Carlos Williams. Copyright 1938 by New Directions Publishing Corporation.
Charles Scribner's Sons, for excerpts from Ernest Hemingway, "A Very Short Story," in *In Our Time*. Copyright 1923, 1930 by Charles Scribner's Sons; copyright renewed 1953, 1958 by Ernest Hemingway. (New York: Charles Scribner's Sons, 1930).
Viking Penguin Inc., for "Eveline" from *Dubliners* by James Joyce. Copyright © 1967 by the Estate of James Joyce.
Gary Snyder, for "All through the rains" from *Riprap*. Copyright © 1959 by Gary Snyder (Ashland, Mass.: Origin Press, 1959).
"Narration and Narrativity in Film and Fiction" originally appeared in slightly different form under the title "Narration and Narrativity in Film" in the *Quarterly Review of Film Studies* (August 1976), copyright © 1976 by Redgrave Publishing Company, P.O. Box 67, South Salem, New York 10590.

Library of Congress Cataloging in Publication Data

Scholes, Robert E.
    Semiotics and interpretation.
Bibliography: p.
    Includes index.
    1. Criticism.   2. Semiotics and literature.
1. Title.
PN98.S46S3   808'.00141   81-15971
ISBN 0-300-02798-2   AACR2
        0-300-03093-2 (pbk.)

10 9 8 7 6 5 4 3 2

I want to dedicate this book to the teachers in whose classrooms my interest in poetics and semiotics was both stimulated and tested:

Miss Jennings, who taught an unwilling and ungrateful boy not only the texts of Caesar, Cicero, and Vergil, but the rudiments of grammar and rhetoric as well.

George Kubler, who convinced me that the history of art was more than mere chronology and introduced me to the work of *his* teacher, Henri Focillon.

René Wellek, who patiently shepherded a flock of football players through the great Russian novels and managed to convey some hints of the formal method to semiliterates like myself.

W. R. Keast, who first made the distinction between matter and manner clear for me, and the history of criticism intelligible—the best seminar leader I have ever seen.

R. S. Crane, who both demonstrated and demanded the most rigorous analysis of fictional form I ever encountered in the classroom.

M. H. Abrams, who helped me to see poetic modes and genres more clearly, and whose critiques of excessive systematizing still worry me.

William M. Sale, Jr., who made the social and cultural matrix of fiction palpable and all narrow formalisms untenable; he set a standard for responsibility that still serves me as an ideal.

My thanks to you all and to all the others, who so often in my case gave better than they got.

CONTENTS

PREFACE

This book is intended as a companion piece to my earlier study, *Structuralism in Literature* (Yale, 1974), but it differs from its predecessor in a number of respects. The study of structuralism was primarily theoretical, and its individual chapters were mainly devoted to discussions of the contributions certain Continental writers had made to the development of structuralism as an intellectual position. This book, on the other hand, is mainly demonstrative, and most of its individual chapters are concerned with particular texts and the ways they may be read or interpreted.

The texts studied include poems, stories, films, a scene from a play, bumper stickers, and a portion of the human anatomy. The approach used throughout is to some extent impressionistic and personal, because this is inevitable in the interpretation of individual texts, but insofar as these interpretations are united by a common methodology, that methodology is semiotic and is often specifically indebted to a range of writers in the semiotic tradition of literary studies. I shall mention these writers and acknowledge some other forms of indebtedness before concluding this preface, but first it will be well to say something about semiotics.

Usually defined as the study of signs (from a Greek root meaning *sign*), semiotics has in fact become the study of codes: the systems that enable human beings to perceive certain events or entities *as* signs, bearing meaning. These systems are themselves parts or aspects of human culture, though subject to constraints of biological and physical sorts as well. (Human speech is limited by human vocal and aural capacities, and by the behavior of sounds in atmosphere, but each human language is peculiar to a specific historical culture.)

As an emerging field or discipline in liberal education, semiotics situates itself on the uneasy border between the humanities and the social sciences, where it is often perceived as too rigid by humanists and too lax by social scientists. Its founding fathers—Ferdinand de Saussure in linguistics and Charles S. Peirce in philosophy—were brilliant innovators, each of whom had a powerful streak of eccentricity in his makeup. In his later years Saussure began to find in texts hidden messages—"anagrams"—that no one else could perceive. Peirce was addicted to opium and to terminology, producing systems of thought beyond the grasp of most other mortals. Yet these two men had truly fertile minds, and the "semiotic" developed by Peirce, along with the "sémiologie" projected by Saussure, have led toward a discipline that seems blessed by their creativity, though threatened with their oddity as well.

This new field of study has one interface with literature, and that is the one I attempt to explore. All human utterances are enabled and limited by systems or codes that are shared by all who make and understand such utterances. If the English language is one such system, it is not the only one. Within English, legal discourse and medical discourse have their own rules, which involve not only the interpretation of messages but also the establishment of who is entitled to utter them and who may act upon them. A prescription must be encoded by a physician and decoded for action by a pharmacist, and these rules are parts of the discourse of medicine. The media or physical systems by which messages are conveyed also influence what can be conveyed in them—not so much as Marshall McLuhan claimed, but in very real and important ways. Literary texts are both produced and interpreted through the mediation of generic codes as well as through language itself. And there are other codes that influence less premeditated forms of utterance. Casual expressions of a very "simple" sort may in fact be governed by both conscious and unconscious impulses toward communication. If everyday life has its "psychopathology," as Freud so eloquently argued, we can perceive this and interpret the speech of the unconscious only when we understand the codes that govern unconscious utterance.

As the study of codes and media, semiotics must take an interest in ideology, in socioeconomic structures, in psychoanalysis, in poetics, and in the theory of discourse. Historically, its development has been powerfully influenced by French structuralism and poststructuralism: that is, by the structural anthropology of Claude Lévi-Strauss, by the neo-Marxism of Louis Althusser, by the "archeology" of Michel Foucault, by the neo-Freudianism of Jacques Lacan, and by the grammatology of Jacques Derrida. An interesting book could be written discussing these important figures, and, indeed, an excellent one has appeared, in which most of them are considered very acutely: *Structuralism and Since*. But my purpose here is to do something different. I wish to show what happens when a practicing semiotician enters the traditional domain of literary interpretation.

There are a number of risks involved in this project, beyond the elementary one that the job may not be done very well. One is that the semiotician's interest in collective structures—genres, discourses, codes, and the like—will cause the uniqueness of the literary text to be lost. Another is that, by entering the domain of "reading" as such, the critic will so fall under the weight of interpretive practice or the spell of personal response that any consistent *semiotic* methodology will be lost in the exegetical tangle. I have tried to guard against these dangers, but I am not certain I have always succeeded. Nor have I even attempted to cover all the literary forms or to illustrate all the things that can be done to literary works in the name of semiotics.

One of the great temptations to which semioticians succumb more often than others is that of terminology. Two others are the use of logical or algebraic symbols and the deployment of elaborate diagrams. I have reduced this paraphernalia to a minimum—in some cases to zero. And I have done this not merely in deference to the gentle reader, but because I have a low tolerance for these things myself. I know how the eyes can begin to glaze over at the appearance of a huge tree diagram on the page. My feeling is that the great usefulness of semiotics to literary studies will not be found in its elaborate analytical taxonomies, but rather is to be derived from a small number of its most basic and powerful concepts, ingeniously applied.

The most elementary terms of Saussure and Peirce (Saussure's signification and value, for instance, or Peirce's icon, index, and symbol) have proved the most useful. In literary semiotics, Jakob-

son's six-part diagram of a fundamental act of communication has
proved immensely fruitful—not because six features are all that
can be discerned in human communication, but because six are
about all we can handle analytically, because they are so clearly
differentiated, and because in Jakobson's hands they are immediately used to make important and interesting distinctions among
major modes of discourse. I refer to Jakobson's diagram again
and again, so that certain chapters might even be called variations
on a theme by Roman Jakobson. The contemporary semiotics of
literature is founded on Jakobson's work. The select bibliography
appended to this book will give fuller citations, but I should like to
mention here those other members of the international community
of literary semioticians upon whom I have leaned most heavily in
undertaking the demonstrations that follow: Roland Barthes, Gérard Genette, Julia Kristeva, and Tzvetan Todorov in Paris, Umberto Eco in Italy, Yuri Lotman and Boris Uspensky in the Soviet
Union, and Seymour Chatman and Michael Riffaterre in the
United States.

It will be apparent to all who read on that I am concerned with
the interpretation of literary texts not simply as an end in itself, but
as an aspect of liberal education. Interpretation—"reading" in the
large sense—is one of the great goals of humanistic study, and the
reading of literary texts is one of the best methods—perhaps *the*
best—of developing interpretive skill in students. Without continually insisting on this argument, I intend my demonstrations and
discussions in the following chapters to enhance the case for the
role of semiotic studies in the teaching of interpretive competence.
This book is addressed primarily to those who care about such matters: to the men and women who study and teach language and literature, and beyond them to all who care about how these matters
are studied and taught.

The eight chapters that follow are not so rigidly arranged that
they must be read in their order of appearance, but they do follow a
certain pattern. The first two are largely theoretical. In Chapter 1, I
try to situate semiotics in relation to criticism in general and to the
teaching of literature in particular. In Chapter 2, I attempt to define
literature from a semiotic perspective, emphasizing some of the
features of literary texts that will be examined later on. Chapter 3

deals with the interpretation of the short poem, with examples from W. S. Merwin, William Carlos Williams, and Gary Snyder. Chapter 4 develops aspects of the theory of narrative, with brief examples based on several American films. Chapter 5 looks at irony as a source of pleasure in literary texts, with attention to the way ironic coding depends upon both genre and ideology. In Chapter 6, I illustrate how the specific methodologies of Todorov, Genette, and Barthes may be combined for a relatively full analysis of a single short story by James Joyce. In Chapter 7, I employ semiotic methods more freely to analyze a single story by Hemingway, and in Chapter 8, I move from purely literary concerns to examine the way literature and language itself shape and control such a "natural" thing as the human body. Chapter 8 illustrates also the affinity between semiotics and feminism as critical methods, which is based on their common interest in the revelation of hidden codes that shape perception and behavior. Taken as a whole, these studies are meant to illustrate, though not to exhaust, the possibilities of a specifically semiotic approach to the practice of textual interpretation. (Versions of Chapters 1, 2, 4, and 6 have been previously published in, respectively, the *Michigan Quarterly, Critical Inquiry,* the *Quarterly Review of Film Studies,* and the *James Joyce Quarterly.*)

My debts are many and it is a pleasure to acknowledge them here. I have mentioned some already and will be more specific about such written sources in the bibliography. My teachers are acknowledged in the dedication. Here I wish to mention those friends and colleagues whose conversation has stimulated, enriched, encouraged, or corrected my thinking on the materials presented in the body of this book. My collaborator in various pedagogical and compositional ventures, Nancy R. Comley, had an important share in developing the interpretation of Williams's "Nantucket" in Chapter 3 and the Hemingway story in Chapter 7. Her essay on Hemingway in *Novel* (vol. 12, no. 3, pp. 244–53) also helped. My colleagues in the Brown University Program in Semiotic Studies, Michael Silverman and Mary Ann Doane, have focused my thinking in many ways, especially by argument. Useful trains of thought and various forms of criticism and encouragement were provided by Carol Holly-Handelman, Kathe D. Finney, Marlena Corcoran, Kaja Silverman, Gayatri C. Spivak, Mark Spilka, Richard Pearce, Michelle Massé, Gregory Benford, Barbara Herrnstein Smith, Sandra Gilbert, Susan Gubar, and Jo Ann S. Putnam-Scholes. An anonymous reader for the Yale University Press provided a sympathetic, acute, and searching critique of the entire manuscript, which led me to make substantial revisions. The early chapters and research were supported by the John Simon Guggenheim Foundation. My thanks to all.

R.S.

June 1981

1
THE HUMANITIES, CRITICISM, AND SEMIOTICS

The humanities may be defined as those disciplines primarily devoted to the study of texts. As the physical sciences concentrate on the study of natural phenomena, and the social sciences on the behavior of sentient creatures, the humanities are connected by their common interest in communicative objects, or texts. Human beings are text-producing animals, and those disciplines called "humanities" are primarily engaged in the analysis, interpretation, evaluation, and production of texts. Where there are texts, of course, there are rules governing text production and interpretation. These sets of rules or customs, with their physical or cultural constraints—variously described as languages, media, codes, genres, discourses, and styles—may also become the objects of humane study. It is worth noting, however, that because the study of texts themselves is privileged in the humanities, the study of codes governing text production and interpretation is often resisted as "nonhumanistic," if not inhumane. This is understandable, but it is a position that becomes less tenable with the growth in our knowledge of the processes governing the encoding and decoding of texts.

Still, it must be acknowledged that our familiar distinctions among the physical sciences, social sciences, and humanities are not merely the jurisdictional boundaries between those political fictions we call "departments." There are major differences of methodology which divide the great fields of study, and these differences are themselves rooted in the nature of the materials studied and the temperaments and abilities of those people who are drawn to each field. The interpretive skills shown by the best students of artistic texts involve tacit and intuitive procedures which

1

have proved highly resistant to systematization and hence difficult to transmit in any direct and formal way. Yet they lie at the center of humanistic study because the artistic text is (by cultural definition) the most valuable text, for its own sake, produced by any human culture, and therefore the text that encourages or requires the most study and interpretation.

Setting aside many difficult and interesting questions (such as the relationships among artistic, religious, and legal texts—and their interpretation), I wish to concentrate here on the situation of literary interpretation at the present time. That is, taking the literary text as representative of all the texts studied by humanists, I wish to consider what advice and examples are currently being offered us for the study of literary texts. And throughout my inquiry I shall try to keep in mind four of the possible social roles that we may currently adopt in relation to such texts: author, critic, teacher, and student. Obviously, the same individual may play any or all of these roles in relation to literary texts—but not at the same time in relation to the same text.

These four roles or functions can be arranged in a regular pattern or syntagm, the elements of which always appear in the same order in relation to any particular text: author, critic, teacher, student. The author produces a primary text. The critic produces a secondary text which is evaluative or interpretive of the primary text. The teacher also produces secondary texts, some of which are ephemeral because they are delivered orally in the classroom, and some of which—in the form of handouts, written assignments, and tests—take a more durable form. Finally, the student produces texts, too, either in the form of oral discussion or as written documents prepared in response to assignments or examination questions.

The syntagmatic chain I have described takes us into the heart of a procedure which is essential to humanistic pedagogy. As professional educators we are all situated in a socioeconomic structure in which our livelihood is dependent upon our functioning in this particular syntagm. And at times we have played—and may play again—any one of the four roles in relation to any particular text. For most of us, however, the two extreme roles are not so likely as the two central ones. That is, we are not likely to be authors of primary texts or students whose responses to the primary texts are guided by instructional assignments. We are all, however, teachers, and on some occasions most of us perform as critics also, whether we publish our critical responses or simply recount them to friends and colleagues. The same person, indeed, is often at different times both critic and teacher with respect to the same text. But the functions are not the same.

In a sense, both critic and teacher aim at eliminating their roles in some way. The critic, having had a say about a particular text, hopes that later interpretations will assimilate that "say," incorporating it into an interpretive tradition. Thus the critic expects to move on perpetually from one text to another. Attempts by critics to assert ownership over texts are misguided at best and ludicrous or obscene at worst. Similarly, the teacher expects to move on perpetually from one student to another. Ideally, this should happen when the student has assimilated the interpretive or evaluative strategies of a particular teacher and can apply them himself (or herself). In practice, we often fail to achieve this end, but we must still hold to it as an aim. This whole process is justified only by the extent to which the student can finally eliminate both teacher and critic in order to become a critical reader of a wide variety of texts.

In considering the state of critical thinking today, I wish to keep this simple pedagogical process in mind while asking two questions. First: What, if anything, have we learned about textual interpretation that has direct implications for pedagogical practice? And second: What specific interpretive attitudes and strategies that are currently active offer us the best models for the interpretation of literary texts?

We may believe that we know all kinds of things about the pedagogy of textual interpretation, but many of our "beliefs" contradict one another or defy all attempts at demonstration. If we set aside all our supposed knowledge, however, and search, in the manner of Descartes, for a fundamental principle for humanistic study, we find not a "cogito" but a "scribo." This at least is what all the modern critical theories can agree upon. I am a humanist not because I think, still less because I read, but because I write— because, finally, I produce texts. Behind the verbal persiflage of Roland Barthes on behalf of the writerly text, behind the

grammatological convolutions of Derridean deconstructivism, behind the aphoristic barrier that is the discourse of Michel Foucault,
behind the deceptive depths and opaque surfaces of Jacques Lacan's insistence on the letter, and more explicitly in the writings of
many Anglo-American critics—we can find one, and perhaps only
one, common principle, and that is the principle of *scribo, ergo
sum.* I produce texts, therefore I am, and to some extent I am the
texts that I produce.

In terms of the simple pedagogical model I have been discussing,
this means that the process of interpretation is not complete until
the student has produced an interpretive text of his or her own.
This is perhaps the place where psychoanalysis has the most to
teach literary pedagogy. Both Freud and Lacan stress the importance of the patient's "putting into words of the event" (Jacques
Lacan, *The Language of the Self*, [Baltimore, 1968], p. 16) in order
for any therapeutic effect to be obtained. It is never enough simply
to tell the patient what must have happened, to raise his consciousness, so to speak. The patient must verbalize for himself. As Freud
and Breuer put it in 1893, "The psychical process which originally
took place must be repeated as vividly as possible; it must be
brought back to its *status nascendi* and then given verbal utterance" (Standard Edition, II, 6, quoted in Wilden's notes to Lacan,
p. 103). I am not suggesting that psychoanalysis and literary interpretation are the same thing, or even that they are highly
analogous processes—only that psychoanalysis has demonstrated
consistently for over three-quarters of a century that there is a significant difference between the states of consciousness involved in
receiving a text and producing one. Specifically, the text we produce is ours in a deeper and more essential way than any text we
receive from outside. When we read we do not possess the text we
read in any permanent way. But when we make an interpretation
we do add to our store of knowledge—and what we add is not the
text itself but our own interpretation of it. In literary interpretation
we possess only what we create.

I hope I am saying nothing new here, only articulating what
every teacher of literature has always known: that it is no use *giving* students interpretations; that they must make them for themselves; that the student's productivity is the culmination of the

pedagogical process. Without this productivity, in fact, the process of humanistic education is incomplete. This is something often overlooked in academic institutions that adopt or try to adopt models from the world of manufacture and commerce. If a school is a factory, then the administrators are "managers," the teachers are "workers," and the students are turned out as "products." Thus, the more students turned out, the higher the productivity of the teachers and the better the management of the administrators. From a certain limited point of view, this is perfectly accurate. What it ignores, of course, is the productivity of the students. The first thing sacrificed in the processing of large numbers of students is the productivity of the students themselves: their production of texts. And since such productivity is the essence of their humanistic training it is the one thing that cannot be sacrificed without damaging the students *as products*. Doubtless TV sets could be produced more quickly and cheaply if those awkward picture tubes could be left out.... Unfortunately, products of a humanistic education with the humane essence left out are less easy to detect than TV sets lacking picture tubes. But the loss to society is real and will take its toll.

I digress, but digression is often a feature of humanistic discourse. To pick up the thread, contemporary critical theory tends to confirm our intuitions about the importance of the production of texts by students of literature. The student must produce interpretive discourse to complete the process of literary study. This raises two subsidiary questions: *How?* and *What kind?* The answer to *How?* falls, I believe, into the area of what we *know* about literary study, and I will therefore discuss it first. The answer to *What kind?* is more controversial and will best be saved for later.

All the modern schools of criticism, however much they disagree about many things, accept the notion that the production of texts involves the acceptance of rules that are already in place. That is, one does not simply learn English and acquire the ability to produce any kind of text in the English language. To acquire a first language is to enter an elaborate cultural situation. Such an event may in itself be traumatic and will in any case have important effects on perception and cognition. To produce texts in a language, moreover, involves accepting a second level of cultural constraints: the codes that govern the stylistic possibilities open to any particular type of discourse. This, too, because it involves a sacrifice of freedom for the sake of obtaining a power, may have its traumatic dimension. We call our studies "disciplines" for the very good reason that they require precisely this sort of sacrifice and submission. The power to speak at all depends upon our giving up the entropic freedom of noise in order to manipulate a small number of phonemes in a conventional way. Similarly, the power to produce any particular kind of discourse—such as that of literary interpretation—requires an acceptance of the conventions of that discourse. The question I am raising now is simply that of the best way to accomplish this for the student of literature.

What is immensely clear is that our practice is presently not in conformity with our knowledge on this point. We have been behaving as if we thought it possible simply to read a text and then produce interpretive discourse about it by inspection and intuition. But we *know* better. And here again the most disparate and mutually disputatious schools of critical thought tend toward agreement. We know that both inspection and intuition are *already* the products of discourse. We read as we have been taught to read and until we have been taught to look for certain things we will not see them. And we write—always and inevitably—on the basis of the models of writing we have already encountered. The ability to be "creative," whether in the discourse of criticism or in the discourse of poetry, is not given to the novice but is earned by mastering the conventions to the point where improvisation becomes possible and power finally is exchangeable for freedom once again.

In short, the student who is properly expected to produce interpretive discourse must be exposed to models of such discourse as well as to the literary texts that will become the subject of interpretation. It is even easier and more reasonable to ask a student to interpret poem X in the manner of critic Y than to ask the same student to simply look at the poem and into his or her own heart and write. This latter request, which seems so reasonable and natural, is in fact much harder and more perverse than the apparently artificial one proposed first. This is so because the novice student, like the novice poet, has no "heart" to speak of, for what we are talking about here is not some ontological essence but a discursive quality, a function of style. Behind the tired trope which urges that the style is the man lurks a great truth: in any form of discourse a personality is achieved only through style. And style is a way of perceiving as well as a way of uttering. If we ask students prematurely to achieve a discursive personality of their own, we force upon them the fraudulent disguising of other voices as their own—whether the voice be that of Cliff, the maker of notes, or of some other explicator or teacher. It is far better to foreground this ventriloqual effect and let them work openly in an intertextual way, while learning from the manner in which these borrowed garments squeeze and stretch the contours of their own discursive personalities.

To put this as simply as possible, our knowledge of the processes of discourse suggests that students who are expected to produce interpretive texts must be given such texts to read so that they can absorb the customs and principles that govern this kind of discourse. This is not to say that if we expect students to interpret text A we must give them what critics X, Y, and Z have said about it; rather, it is to urge that the student will be in a much better position to write about text A if the curriculum includes some examples of critics X, Y, and Z interpreting texts A1, A2, and A3, which are similar in structure or style to text A. This is how we all learn, so this is how we must teach. It is that simple.

What is not so simple is *what kind* of interpretive texts we, as teachers, should provide as models and encourage our students to produce. Here contemporary critical theory seems to offer a bewildering and contradictory array of possibilities. In the remainder of this discussion I shall try to put these theories and their associated practices into an intelligible scheme, and to make some recommendations based on this scheme. In doing so I must disclose my own predilections at the outset, for we are no longer in an area where it is reasonable to speak of knowledge. Fundamental issues are in doubt here, as hardly ever before. My approach to literary study—and indeed to many other things—is one that I call semiotic, and I will locate and discuss it in its proper place. I mention it now because the scheme I am going to use as an organizing principle is a semiotic one, based on the simple description of an act of communication popularized by Roman Jakobson. In this description, which can be diagramed, Jakobson distinguishes six elements present in any act of communication. Adjusting this diagram to describe the reading of a literary text, we get something like this:

$$\text{author} \underline{\qquad \begin{array}{c} \text{contexts} \\ \text{text} \end{array} \qquad} \text{reader}$$
$$\begin{array}{c} \text{medium} \\ \text{codes} \end{array}$$

The active schools of critical theory and interpretation can be ordered, at least in a preliminary way, by their emphasis of particular features of this diagram. That is, if we take the reading of a literary text as a complete act of communication, each school of criticism tends to privilege one of the elements at the expense of others in its attitude toward the reading process. Further refinements come in the variety of attitudes it is possible to take toward the privileged element, in the connections seen among the various elements, and so on. But let us begin to locate some critical schools and see how this scheme works. We can start with the extremes, which are clearest.

At present, we have vigorous advocates of both author-oriented and reader-oriented criticism. By author-oriented criticism I mean interpretation that privileges the role of the author in the text, and seeks to recover the authorial intention as the key to a text's meaning. The principal advocate of this approach is E. D. Hirsch, who has argued his case with energy and eloquence in two books: *Validity in Interpretation* and *The Aims of Interpretation*. Supported by the work of the Speech-Act philosophers, Hirsch has argued—and in my view very persuasively—that we cannot speak of a determinate interpretation at all unless we postulate an authorial intention to govern that interpretation. Hirsch's approach is in fact the most conservative way of arriving at the meaning of a text. It assumes that the author of a literary text is by definition superior to the reader and that his achievement has been equal to his intention. Thus, the burden is on the reader to recover that intention. This is an orderly approach; in fact, it is a kind of law-and-order approach. It offers principles for the validation of interpretation and thus lends itself to a certain kind of pedagogy. As Hirsch reminds us, this tradition of hermeneutic study has its roots in biblical exegesis, so we should not be surprised to find that it tends to regard the author as God. Its most powerful appeal, I should think, comes to our sense that students are in fact not adequate readers, and hence are in need of a rigorous discipline in which there must be a standard for "right" and "wrong" readings. Obviously, there is an ideology as well as a pedagogy implied here, and it may not be easy to separate the two. But it is clear that the strength of this approach lies in its order and that its danger comes from the same source. It can lead to a rigid authoritarianism that may stifle the student's creative impulses and make reading a chore, or worse, an occasion for fear and hostile defensiveness.

At the other extreme we have a critical school that emphasizes the reader and privileges the reader's response to the text. Readers *make* meaning, argue the proponents of this school, and should have the right to make any meaning that their own psychic needs require of a particular text. In this view not order but disorder seems to be privileged. As the editor of *Reader: A Newsletter of Reader-Oriented Criticism and Teaching* put it recently, "The reader must be thought of as essentially free to create the text." In this lively new journal, the freedom and creativity of the reader are emphasized, and a veritable anarchy of interpretive variation is encouraged. The possibility of misreading or misinterpretation is ignored. From the point of view of pedagogy, I can only say that it must be a happy teacher indeed who feels that his or her students can make no mistakes in reading. But any teacher who has ever confronted the real problems of cultural deprivation, which produce readers of gravely limited capabilities, must feel that the position that readers make meaning is a luxurious attitude which most classrooms cannot afford. And in point of fact the classrooms of reader-oriented critics often take a form familiar to us from the sixties: where a "facilitator" has replaced the "teacher" and offers students a freedom which they soon perceive as illusory, if not fraudulent. But surely in the teaching of literary interpretation there must be some middle ground between the anarchy of reader-emphasis, which declines the pedagogical gambit altogether, and the authoritarianism of author-emphasis, which may well stifle creativity.

Surely, there is, and we will find some varieties of it in the center of the Jakobsonian diagram. Criticism that emphasizes the text itself has been at the center of American critical thought until the past decade. For the New Criticism, as it came to be called, clearly repudiated both the relevance of the author's intention to the interpretation of a text and the reader's freedom to make any kind of interpretive gesture that seemed congenial. This is one reason why *Understanding Poetry* and its derivatives became such staples of our classrooms for such a long time. The New Criticism offered an exercise of textual ingenuity supported by the dictionary and grammar book in place of the alternatives of authorial domination or an anarchy of readers. Ideologically, this placed the New Criticism in the American tradition of constitutional interpretation—a legalistic exegesis rather than a biblical hermeneutics—which offered the interpreter considerable exercise of ingenuity, but within fairly rigid rules as to what was relevant and what was not. We hire lawyers to make our intentions *textually* ironclad. Poetic texts work differently, as the New Critics demonstrated very well, but like wills, legal codes, or the Constitution itself, they were to be taken as documents entirely sufficient to proclaim their own meaning. What Wordsworth and Jefferson said outside the text was to be considered irrelevant.

This position, which proved fruitful in the classroom and in the study, is less vigorous today, partly because it has been assimilated and partly because of cogent assaults on it from various quarters. Hirsch has shown that the "intentional fallacy" does not eliminate the need to consider intention in determining meaning. And the scholars have had their revenge, demonstrating that ignorance of period styles and usages, or of bibliographical methods of text establishment, can make for ludicrous interpretive errors. Similarly, the Marxists and other sociocritics have shown how ideology and cultural matrices cannot be ignored in textual interpretation. Historical scholarship and sociocriticism both, of course, emphasize context in their approaches to literary texts, insisting that meaning is not simply "in" the words but in a set of values and implications which are matters of history and must be so understood.

From early on in this country the New Critics were also opposed by the Neo-Aristotelians, who emphasized rhetorical and generic

criticism, interpreting texts in the light of generic norms and conventions: codes in Jakobson's sense of the word. There were other
differences between these two schools, of course, and a major one
was the tendency of the Chicago school of rhetorical critics to see
texts as primarily to be interpreted in terms of their ethical or emotional powers of persuasion, the text coercing the reader on behalf
of the author; while the New Haven critics saw a more active
reader exploring literary texts which were marked by an ambiguity
or irony that finally short-circuited or undercut any clearly persuasive intention. The later developments of this opposition are interesting, and we shall be returning to them. For the moment we
must pause to note that the New Critical emphasis on the text included the assumption that poetic texts are designed to produce a
peculiarly poetic response: the ambiguity of the text is an objective
correlative of a purely contemplative state in the reader, who rec-
ognizes that the text is not seeking to denote a reality but to con-
note an elegantly balanced esthetic structure. Thus, in New Critical thought the text was as isolated as possible from the other features of communication, and every text was as isolated as possible
from every other text, in a Crocean uniqueness. The text was not
just a text but a "work." Both the strengths and the weaknesses of
New Critical interpretation stem from this extreme focus on the
work as a uniquely meaningful object.

On a superficial examination the Russian formalists appear to
have shared many critical assumptions with the New Critics. They
too emphasized texts and insisted that any worldly context or persuasive purpose could not be of major importance in a poetic text.
Their views are fairly compressed into Jakobson's notion that a
poetic text is one which emphasizes its own textual form. The formalists differed from the New Critics, however, in their extreme
interest in devices and conventions of poetic structure. They always sought the poetic in poetry and the prosaic in prose, so that
even their studies of individual texts always came to turn on a point
of poetic principle that could be applied to other texts in the same
genre. Thus, their interpretive strategies tended to move from an
emphasis on texts to an emphasis on the codes that govern the production of texts. This emphasis is even more pronounced in the
structuralist descendants of Russian formalism, and has led in

many structuralists to a privileging of those texts that are obviously dominated by codes and conventions: folk literature and popular film and fiction.

The formalist and structuralist emphasis on codes has led to the development of a semiotic approach to literary study that has proved quite compatible with the rhetorical approach of our own Chicago Aristotelians. It makes a good deal of sense, for instance, to see Gérard Genette's *Discours du récit* (translated as *Narrative Discourse*) as a development of Wayne Booth's *Rhetoric of Fiction* (Chicago, 1961), and Seymour Chatman's recent *Story and Discourse* is also in this newly unified tradition, which emphasizes an approach to texts through generic codes and stylistic conventions. Other semiotic studies of recent years confirm a sense of rapprochement between European and American critical approaches to interpretation. Yuri Lotman's *Analysis of the Poetic Text* and Michael Riffaterre's *Semiotics of Poetry* approach poems through conventions and codes but share with the New Critics a sense of the poetic text as largely self-referential rather than oriented to a wordly context. Barbara Herrnstein Smith's *Poetic Closure* (Chicago, 1968) also concentrates on codes and conventions as a way into the interpretation of texts. But her willingness to speak of a poem's "sense of truth" links her to the Chicago critics, whose interest in genres and codes has always been tempered with a concern for the emotional *and* intellectual impact of a text on readers.

It is precisely this impact that worries a semiotic critic like Roland Barthes and helps to account for a book like *S/Z*, in which Barthes subverts the traditional distinction between popular and classical texts. As a structuralist, Barthes privileged popular and mythic texts in his interpretive essays. In his poststructuralist phase, Barthes has tried to show that the classic text is just as unoriginal as the popular, just as dominated by received opinions and formulaic gestures. Realism, Barthes tells us, has nothing to do with reality; it is simply a text that is readable because it is composed entirely of what is already known. The classic realistic text is a tissue of clichés. Because all codes are finally coercive. Barthes denounces the readable text in *S/Z*, and asks for a writable text, a text that is sufficiently free of logic and grammar to allow the reader to take an active role in textualization: to "write."

For Barthes the classic text is all too readable, its rich fabric of interlocking codes forcing upon the interpreter a role of passive consumption from which only an unreadable text offers any hope of freedom. But Barthes's own practice and that of the school of critics now called "deconstructivist" suggest that there is an alternative to this abhorrently passive role. American deconstructivist criticism may be seen as stemming from Paul de Man's commentary in *Blindness and Insight* (Oxford, 1971) on Jacques Derrida's *Grammatology*. This critical school saves the reader from passivity by assuming that virtually every text has "areas of blindness" that are in some way crucial to its interpretation. The text cannot say all it means, because its meanings are enabled by its silence on some crucial point. From here it is but a step to Harold Bloom's insistence that every poem is based on a misreading by the poet of a predecessor's work (see *The Anxiety of Influence*[Oxford, 1973], passim), and to other strategies that free the reader from passivity by postulating imperfection or inadequacy in the text. The great virtue of this attitude is that it allows for concentration on the text while encouraging a creative role for the critical reader. It neutralizes the hermeneutic insistence on the intention of the author by assuming that this intention will itself be clouded by bad faith or blindness on the author's part. As de Man says, it affirms "the absolute dependence of the interpretation on the text and of the text on the interpretation" (p. 141).

This balanced position, however, is not easy to maintain, for a variety of reasons. On the one hand, by weakening the role of authorial intention in the text, deconstructivist criticism opens the way to extremes of "readerism," in which texts are accused of "total indeterminacy" (see *Reader;* no. 5, p. 7). And on the other hand, context-oriented critics are quick to provide explanations for blindness that lead to interpretation according to particular formulas. Specifically, Marxist critics will attribute blindness to ideological blinkers and interpret according to their own dogmas; and psychoanalytic critics will find that the notion of "blindness" is easily translatable into the vocabulary of "repression" and "sublimation." This is why there is so much infighting among the followers of Derrida and those of Lacan at the present time. To deconstruct a text according to a Freudian formula, or even according to the subtler methods of Lacan, is not at all what de Man and Derrida had in mind. It is not, in fact, deconstruction at all, because it is so centered in a discipline that pretends to knowledge. Your true deconstructivist sees interpretation as a perpetual exposure of blindnesses, just as your true Maoist sees the revolution as a perpetual decentering of the social structure. Both of these views imply the happy corollary that critics and revolutionaries will never be out of business.

Let me try to be more precise, now, in situating a semiotic approach to literature among these other approaches. Semiotics rejects authoritarian hermeneutics through its critique of the notion of author. For the semiotic critic an author is neither a god contemplating his creation nor even a fully unified individuality freely making esthetic choices. The producers of literary texts are themselves creatures of culture, who have attained a human subjectivity through language. What they produce as literary text is achieved by their acceptance of the constraints of generic or discursive norms. Through them speak other voices—some cultural and public, some emerging distorted from those aspects of private need repressed as the price for attaining a public subjectivity in language. An author is not a perfect ego but a mixture of public and private, conscious and unconscious elements, insufficiently unified for use as an interpretive base.

Readers, of course, are similarly constructed: divided psyches traversed by codes. Leaving the reader "free" to interpret is an impossibility. The "free" reader is simply at the mercy of the cultural codes that constitute each person *as* a reader, and of the manipulative features of the text, the classroom, and the whole reading situation as well. A major function of this book will be to develop and illustrate a semiotic position on the teaching of reading. For the moment, it will suffice to say that instruction in reading must both socialize and desocialize. That is, students need to acquire the interpretive codes of their culture, but they also need to see them *as* codes, so that they can appreciate those texts that reshape accepted ideas and at the same time defend themselves against the manipulative exploitation of received opinion.

In distinguishing a semiotic approach to literary study from others it is probably most important to make a clear division between semiotic analysis and its major predecessor in American critical thought and pedagogy: the New Criticism. This distinction can be based upon the difference between the notions of "work" and "text." New Critical exegesis is based on the notion of the literary "work": a complete, self-sufficient object, constructed of words on a page, that should yield its meanings to anyone trained in practical criticism. The boundedness of "works" is their distinguishing characteristic. They are to be seen as free of authorial intention, free of historical necessity, and free from the reader's projections of value and meaning. Meaning is folded into the words on the page and must be drawn out by a skilled unfolder of such meanings.

This New Critical privileging of the integrity of the work in literary study led to a whole series of interpretive, pedagogical, and editorial gestures. Students were given poems to interpret with their titles removed, their author's names concealed, and their dates ignored. Anthologies were produced with the works ordered not by chronology but by the alphabet, with biographical information omitted or hidden in appendices, with no visible clues as to country or date of origin. In the name of improved interpretation, reading was turned into a mystery and the literature classroom into a chapel where the priestly instructor (who knew the authors, dates, titles, biographies, and general provenance of the texts) astounded the faithful with miracles of interpretation. The scandal at the heart of the New Criticism—and the source of its power—was this use of cultural codes by instructors who officially asserted that such material was irrelevant to the interpretive process. I am not suggesting conscious fraud, of course, but a myth of pedagogy that was believed because it gratified the pedagogues who believed in it. And the whole position was grounded in the notion of the bounded, self-sufficient work.

A text, as opposed to a work, is open, incomplete, insufficient. This is not a quality inherent in any particular piece of writing, mind you, but only a way of regarding such a piece of writing or any other combination of signs. The same set of words can be regarded as either a work or a text. As a text, however, a piece of writing must be understood as the product of a person or persons, at a given point in human history, in a given form of discourse, taking its meanings from the interpretive gestures of individual readers using the grammatical, semantic, and cultural codes available to them. A text always echoes other texts, and it is the result of choices that have displaced still other possibilities. The records of this textualizing activity may or may not be available as manuscript drafts, but the process must be assumed anyway. A text is always the result of an arbitrary decision to stop writing at a particular point. The analyst is entitled to speculate about what went on before the decision to stop was made, and what might have gone on afterward: about what is excluded as well as what was included. Treating a piece of writing as a text has other ramifications which I shall be exploring later on in this book as I attempt to go beyond these general statements to specific demonstrations of the semiotic analysis of texts. I trust that I have already made it plain that I am an advocate of semiotic studies. In the pages to come I shall be exploring the range and the limits of semiotics as an academic discipline and a tool of textual analysis.

2

TOWARD A SEMIOTICS OF LITERATURE

"Literature," of course, is a word, not a thing. In casual conversation the word is used in many ways, some of them in conflict with one another. "Literature" may be thought of as true writing versus false, as beautiful writing versus useful, as nontrue writing versus true/false writing, and so on. It can be thought of as consisting of a few established generic forms, such as poem, play, and story, with such debatable genres as the essay and the film lurking on the borders. Most departments of literature function with no better concepts than these, and, as F. E. Sparshott has ironically pointed out (in *Centrum* 3, no. 1 [Spring 1975]: 5–22), they proceed with all the confidence in the world.

To some extent I sympathize with the traditional muddle here. Often what begins as clarification ends as nonsense, producing categories so exclusive or inclusive that they bring all attempts at systematic thinking about literature into disrepute. Muddling along, in literary theory as in life, is often more humane and even more efficient than the alternatives offered by political, ethical, or esthetic systems. We may in fact "know" more than we can systematize about certain kinds of human behavior, so that our intuitions may indeed be superior to our more reasoned positions. And yet, we who study what we call "literature" cannot help but desire to understand better what we are doing. We study in order to know, and the very problem of knowing what literature is makes it attractive to us. My attempt to deal with the problem here is based on the formalist, structuralist, and semiotic tradition of critical thought, but at certain crucial points I shall bend that tradition in what I take to be a necessary direction. Some might even say that I have bent it beyond the breaking point.

The word "literature," I wish to argue, should be used to designate a certain body of repeatable or recoverable acts of communi-cation. Later on I shall elaborate on the "certain" part of the defini-tion, which requires the exclusion of some repeatable or recovera-ble communicative acts from the literary category. But first I must define the other terms in this definition. "Repeatable or recovera-ble" requires that something called literature have a certain dura-bility. This may take the form of a written text, a recorded utter-ance, a reel of film, or something transmitted orally, like a saying, joke, myth, or epic poem. In the oral forms, what is recovered is usually not an identical text but a recognizable structure—the "same" joke or epic poem in different words—but this "same-ness" brings such works within the limits of this definition of litera-ture. A saying or performance that is not recoverable or repeata-ble, whether a forgotten joke or a lost manuscript, may well have been literary, but it is no longer a part of literature, since literature consists of the body of available performances only. It has been argued (by Sparshott among others) that all written texts should be considered literature, and there is some justification for this, as we shall see later on. Writing not only preserves utterances verbatim, it also translates material directly available to the senses into another medium, which, as I shall argue, is an elementary kind of fictionalization.

The word "act" in the definition of literature being proposed here requires that our repeatable or recoverable utterance be a deliber-ate action on the part of some sentient being. A mistake is not liter-ature. But it can be made literature by someone else's performance of it. Any utterance or human gesture can be made literary by its being deliberately incorporated into another utterance. Any trivial or vulgar bit of speech or gesture can function in a literary way in a story or play, for instance, or even in a Joycean "epiphany," just as a piece of driftwood or trash can be incorporated in a work of sculpture, or any found object be turned into visual art by an act of selection and display.

Finally, the word "communication" in the definition must be considered. It has been used here because it includes some non-verbal systems of signification as well as the expected verbal forms. A category termed "literature" which excluded theater and film would be embarrassing and awkward for many reasons, among which is the fact that what is recognizably the same work (Henry James's *Washington Square*, for instance) may exist effectively as a printed text, a stage performance, and a film. The word "communication" may seem to open the way too far to nonverbal forms like mime and dance, which are clearly communicative, and even to all the visual and musical forms of expression. Most music "communicates" something, as does most visual art, though clearly there is a broad range from representational forms to "pure" or abstract forms. Here it may be useful to limit the meaning of communication in this definition to utterances that are reasonably susceptible to verbal restatement or paraphrase. Even so, this will be an untidy border—a point that must be acknowledged here. If the other aspects of this definition and demonstration are sufficiently successful to make this weakness important, then it can be considered more fully upon another occasion. For the moment let it suffice to say that highly iconographic works of visual art as well as vocal and programmatic music are to some extent literary.

More important at the moment is that part of the definition originally masked by the word "certain." What quality, you will wish to know, makes any given communicative act a work of literature? I, like any good Prague school structuralist, will answer, in a word, "literariness." This response, of course, is logically splendid but entirely meaningless until the new term is given a less tautological semantic coding—which will be our business here. The major contribution of Roman Jakobson to literary study was his deliverance of us all from "literature" as an absolute category. "Literariness," he has taught us, is found in all sorts of utterances, some of which are not especially literary. And a "literary work" is simply one in which literariness is dominant. Obviously, this allows for borderline cases and disputation, but this is undoubtedly an advantage, since "literature" as an absolute category always provokes disputation anyway, and by making the argument turn on "literariness," we should at least know what kind of evidence ought to decide such disputes—if, and it is a large "if," we can define "literariness" in a satisfactory way.

It may be, of course, that we need not define literariness as an aspect of utterance at all. One might, in fact, overturn the whole problem by doing as Jonathan Culler suggests in *Structuralist Poetics* and regarding literariness not as a function of the work itself but as a special way of reading. Culler suggests that the issue ought not to be the literariness of the text but the "literary competence" of the reader: "Rather than say, for example, that literary texts are fictional, we might cite this as a convention of literary interpretation and say that to read a text as literature is to read it as fiction" (p. 128). But should the "competent reader" read all texts as fictions or should this person read every text in an appropriate way? Culler suggests that competence is primarily a mastery of generic conventions—a position with which I am in sympathy. But are all conventions literary? Are all texts fictions? These are not simple questions, and much debate could be expended upon them, but in order to settle such debate we should have to face the question of literariness all over again. The problem of litera ɹess will not go away, whether we locate it in the text, the reader, or the system. The solution, I am about to argue, lies in seeing the "literary" as a quality that transforms all the major functions of an act of communication, including the role of the reader—which brings us back to Roman Jakobson.

The six features of a communicative act as popularized in Jakobson's diagram are sender, receiver, contact, message, code, and context.

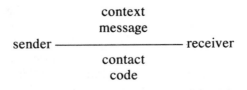

In Jakobson's own formulation the aesthetic function, which makes a verbal expression literary, lies in a transformation of the form of the message itself. A literary utterance may be distinguished from a nonliterary utterance by its emphasis on its own formal structure. This emphasis forces us to consider the utterance as a structured object with a certain density or opacity. It is not a transparent vehicle through which our thoughts are directed to some context or action. It is an entity to be contemplated in its own right. This formulation is closely related to many other views, such as those of I. A. Richards and the New Critics. It rests ultimately on a Kantian assumption about the purposelessness of esthetic objects.

It is in part a useful formulation, but I find it objectionable for a number of reasons. For one, it applies much better to verse, especially to highly formulaic verse, than to prose fiction or drama. For another, it abandons much that has been gained by seeing literariness as a feature of communication rather than as a mode of purposeless activity called "art." For once this notion of art is allowed into the picture, all those aspects of literature which are cognitive or instructive are found to be impurities. If music is the most perfect art, because it refers to nothing, proves nothing, advocates nothing, then literature, which is always referring, arguing, advocating, turns out to be perpetually imperfect. Rather than accept the notion that literature is a kind of failed art, we who have made literary study a central concern of our lives must seek a definition that accounts for this centrality. Seeing literature as a refinement or elaboration of the elements of communication rather than as a vulgarization of the elements of art is the necessary first step in this direction. Jakobson's neat formulation pays too great a price for its neatness. It turns back toward esthetics just when it should continue on with semiotics, and the result is a definition of literariness that excludes many of the most important qualities of all literature, including much poetry. It is time now to move toward a formulation that will yield us a more satisfactory notion of literariness.

Stating it as simply as I can, we sense literariness in an utterance when any one of the six features of communication loses its simplicity and becomes multiple or duplicitous. Let me illustrate this first with some minimal cases. We are all familiar with what happens when we sense a difference between the maker of an utterance and the speaker of it. We say then that the words are those of a "persona" of the author, meaning, as the word implies, that the author has donned a mask. Whenever a communicative act encourages us to sense a difference between maker and speaker, our literary competence has been activated. This is true not only in such obvious situations as when we encounter the words of characters in plays or stories, but in essays also, whenever the essayist

adopts a tone or role that seems to be a deviation from some antici-
pated norm. Even in casual conversation, when a speaker adopts a
particular tone, register, or dialect for a given occasion, we notice
this as a kind of literary behavior. In written prose a device like the
ironic presentation of argument in Swift's "Modest Proposal" is
simply an extreme case of this duplicity of the "sender" of a communication.

Similarly, if the words of an utterance seem to be aimed not directly at us but at someone else, this duplicitous situation is essentially literary. John Stuart Mill emphasized this when he said that
poetry is not heard but overheard. It is perhaps unfortunate, but
situations of eavesdropping and voyeurism are in part literary—
which is no doubt why they figure so prominently in avowed literary texts. The literary competence of readers with respect to this
feature of communicative acts is often a matter of imagining the
person to whom the utterance is addressed or of perceiving meanings that are not intended for, or understood by, the ostensible auditor. Every communicative subtlety requires a corresponding
subtlety of interpretation.

We are placed in a literary situation also when the contact is not
simple. If spoken words are presented to us in writing, for instance,
either the writer or the reader must supply the features of oral
communication lost in this translation—as Laurence Sterne reminds us when he takes such pains to record Corporal Trim's pos-
ture, gesture, and emphasis as the corporal reads a document aloud
in *Tristram Shandy*. Of course by recording in writing the reading
aloud of a written document, Sterne makes the situation doubly
literary with respect to the contact. Similarly, all descriptions of
things normally perceived visually tend toward the literary because they seek to "translate" what would be a visual contact into
a verbal one. The notion that all written documents are "literature" is based on this process. In fact, the more difference we
sense between the verbal contact of print and our normal means of
perception of the objects named in any printed text, the more literary the utterance is likely to be. It is therefore probable that all writing contains at least traces of literariness, but we must remember
that literariness does not equal literature until it dominates any
given utterance.

Duplicity in the form of the message itself, though immensely complicated, is the aspect of literariness that we presently understand best, because it has been most carefully studied. Jakobson and Richards and all the formalists and New Critics have alerted us to the various sound effects and syntactic patternings of verse as well as to the ironies, ambiguities, paradoxes, and other duplicitous features of poetic messages. I do not wish to dwell on these features here except to point out that they function not to cut the work off from the world by making it a self-contained object, as so many theoreticians have argued—rather, they function to create a literary tension between the utterance as communicative and externally referential, on the one hand, and as incommunicative and self-referential, on the other. As Murray Krieger, among others, has argued, a poem usually tantalizes us by being at the same time a mirror and a window.

I have saved the most complicated for last: code and context. We can postpone code even further, since all the features we have been considering as literary may be described in terms of conventions or devices that transform ordinary discourse into literary discourse. These conventions or devices constitute the codes of literature. We shall return to codes and coding, but first we must face the most difficult and interesting problem in literary theory: the problem of context. Jakobson himself removes the problem from the literary sphere, simply saying that an utterance which emphasizes its context is referential, not poetic, and many theoreticians, like Richards, oppose referential discourse to nonreferential as a way of describing the difference between utilitarian and aesthetic texts. Both the formalist and the New Critical schools of criticism tend to deny literary texts any cognitive quality. In terms of the model of communication we are working with, this means denying them access to any context beyond their own verbal system or other texts that share that system. My intention here is to argue for a contrary assumption. And in doing so I must break with a powerful tradition in semiotic studies that runs from Saussure to Barthes and is presently rampant in Parisian structuralism.

The most powerful assumption in French semiotic thought since Saussure has been the notion that a sign consists not of a name and the object it refers to, but of a sound-image and a concept, a signifier and a signified. Saussure, as amplified by Roland Barthes and others, has taught us to recognize an unbridgeable gap between words and things, signs and referents. The whole notion of "sign and referent" has been rejected by the French structuralists and their followers as too materialistic and simpleminded. Signs do not refer to things, they signify concepts, and concepts are aspects of thought, not of reality. This elegant and persuasive formulation has certainly provided a useful critique of naïve realism, vulgar materialism, and various other -isms that can be qualified with crippling adjectives. But it hasn't exactly caused the world to turn into a concept. Even semioticians eat and perform their other bodily functions just as if the world existed solidly around them. The fact that the word "*boulangerie*" has no referent does not prevent them from receiving their daily bread under that sign. As Borges put it: "The world, alas, is real; I, alas, am Borges." Obviously, the whole question of the relationship between words and things cannot be debated here. That language would generate words like "orgasm" or "tonsil" without any assistance from nonverbal experience seems to me highly unlikely. In my view, if language really were a closed system, it would be subject, like any other closed system, to increase in entropy. In fact, it is new input into language from nonverbal experience that keeps language from decaying.

The theory of literature that I am advocating here depends upon our acceptance of the view that an act of communication may indeed point to the phenomenal world and even have the temerity to aim at what may lie behind the wall of phenomena—as *Moby Dick* seeks to tell us something about a real whaling industry and the behavior of real whales and whalers, while also probing deeper into the mysteries of the universe. To accept this view we need not settle any questions about things in themselves, ultimate reality, ideas, or essences. We have only to acknowledge that some correspondence between our thought and the world around us is at least theoretically possible—as in atomic physics, where a mathematical system of signs, interpreted through technology, may lead to the destruction of whole cities and all their citizens.

To isolate literariness in the context of an utterance we need a terminology that will enable us to recognize different aspects of contextual reference. The terminology I wish to offer is based on

three related binary oppositions, or three aspects of a single, ultimate opposition: absent versus present, semiotic versus phenomenal, and abstract versus concrete. A neutral, unliterary context is
present, phenomenal, and concrete. That is, the context is present
to both sender and receiver of a given message. It is there, percep-
tually available to both of them, as free of semiotic coding as possible, and it is more like a thing than like an idea. For instance, if two
people are looking out of a window together and one says, "It is
raining," the context is concrete, phenomenal, and present. If,
however, they open a book and read the words, "It is raining," the
context is still concrete, still potentially phenomenal; and yet, because it is absent, the meaning of the phrase is totally different. The
meaning can no longer be directly referred to the rain outside the
window. It is raining not in present reality but in a space we have
learned to call fictional. To enter fictional space through the
medium of words, we must reverse the processes of perception,
generating the images, sounds, and other perceptual data that
would be available through our senses if we were in the presence of
the named phenomena.

If the same phrase were to occur in a letter, since the sender and
receiver are not present to one another, and therefore not both in
the presence of the phenomenon referred to, the phrase would
again generate a fictional space, and the more the writer tried to
turn the phenomenon of the rain, which only he had perceptual access to, into words, the more concretely that space would be filled
and extended. Any elaborate description of the rain would per-
force become more literary. (It is worth noting that a "description"
that substituted analytical or "scientific" categories for the perceptual categories of human observation would be less literary,
because less concrete. What we mean by "concrete" is "description according to our normal modes of perception." The codes of
fiction are tied to our perceptual system as well as to our language.)

If the letter writer were to begin by describing the rain outside his
window and to end his letter by saying, "When I said it was raining
before, and described all that stuff, it wasn't really raining. I made
all that up"—and if we were to receive that letter and read it, how
would we react? And if he added a postscript in which he asserted
that when he said he had "made up" the rain he was lying? And so

on? The message contradicts itself, aggressively reminding us that we have no access to the context. We can never know whether the writer was looking out a real window at real rain or not. The fictional status of the "rain" does not depend on the fact or nonfact of rain but on the absence of the "real" context from the reader. Any description we read is a fiction. On the relation of such fictions to our "real" context, more later.

A context that is present and phenomenally available does not invite the literary the way an absent context does. In fact, literariness based on a present context is likely to result from some semiotic violation of that context. If one of our rain watchers should say to the other, "Nice weather we're having," this would instantly be perceived by the other as a simple irony. In fact this transaction would be so instantaneous that the complex process involved might be lost. What happens in such a situation is this: A says, "Nice weather." B is aware that the context denies the statement—the phenomenal denies the semiotic. But knowing that A is aware of the actual situation, and that A is aware that he is aware of it, B knows finally that A is referring to a fictional context—where the weather is indeed nice—as a way of signaling his disapproval of the actual phenomenon of this particular rain. It is this complex process of comparing two contexts that allows us to say that the apparent meaning of the phrase is not the real meaning. What we might regard as the "figure" or trope, irony, is in fact a function of context and cannot be determined from the form of the message alone. Upon examination, other figures, which seem to be more purely verbal, like puns and metaphors, will be seen to function by juxtaposition of contrasting contexts rather than at some purely verbal level. Irony, of course, is only the most extreme semiotic violation of present context. Any recoding of the phenomenal will contain some measure of literariness because it changes the contact (as was observed above), and the more such recoding may be recognized as a distortion, the more literary it will seem.

Having seen how fiction results from the semiotic generation of an absent context or the distortion of a present one, we should perhaps pause to consider how such fictions differ from two near relatives, the lie and the mistake. Assume that only one of our characters can actually see out the window, and for reasons of his own he decides to deceive the other person. (Note that the more concrete I make those reasons, the more fictional this scene becomes.) He says it is raining when actually it is not, and he deceives the other into accepting this view. By creating two contexts he has indeed generated a fiction, but his companion, accepting his statement, is aware of a single context only. For this reason there is no fiction. Because she (note how the more specific feminine pronoun further fictionalizes the scene) accepts his translation of the phenomenal into the verbal as purely transparent and referential, she perceives neither fiction nor lie in his statement. For him, of course, it is both a fiction and a lie, that is, a fiction presenting itself as fact with the intent to deceive. For us, eavesdropping on the scene, recognizing the whole thing as an artificial, illustrative context, the scene is entirely fictional, despite its function in this nonfictional discourse.

Similarly, if the person who glances out the window misperceives the phenomenon outside it, reporting rain falling but not deceiving intentionally, this utterance is not a fiction to the speaker but may appear to be one to an auditor who happens to check up on the statement. The natural impulse for such an auditor would be to wonder whether the textual discrepancy should be attributed to a lie or a mistake—and such wondering would require her to fictionalize in order to reach a decision. This is so because all specification or concretization of human motives is presentation of a context that is unavailable, absent, beyond direct perception.

Up to now we have been concerned with the minimally literary. Obviously, things like a single ironic comment about the weather are not likely to be preserved in the annals of literature—but such things look toward more elaborate literary structures. The doubling of contexts is the beginning of the kind of literariness characteristic of fiction. Such doubling opens the way to other literary effects, which depend on the contrasting qualities of the contexts invoked by a particular message. We can find such multicontextuality operating, often with surprising sophistication, at a level of discourse not very far removed from conversations about the weather. I propose to demonstrate this briefly by considering the literary elements of a few bumper stickers that were prominent in our automotive dialogue several years ago.

Take for instance a bumper sticker that says, simply, "Peace." The conventions of bumper sticking enable us to interpret this as a proposition: "The driver of this car is in favor of peace." If the driver happens to drive in a particularly hostile and violent manner, the contrast between the intended verbal message and the behavioral signs may well amuse us. We, spectators to this scene, may put the intended context of the sticker message (some political situation of war or violence) and the unintended revelation of the behavior into a new context of our own. We may mentally fictionalize this situation, inventing a character who says one thing and does another, and so on. But it is our performance that is literary here, not the performance of the sticker owner or the sticker maker.

Take another instance, in which the behavior of the car to which the sticker is attached will be ignored. Imagine a sticker that says "Peace" and bears a picture of a dove. The dove symbolizes peace here mainly by cultural reference to biblical and other texts. It strengthens the word by adding these biblical contexts to the text, perhaps reminding us of the Prince of Peace, and so on. As we bring these cultural contexts to bear on the phenomenal context, some act of war or violence, we perform, again, a minimally literary act. Here, the realities of the political situation against which the sign must be perceived have a powerful effect on our interpretation. A "Peace" sticker had a more concrete and specific context for Americans during the Vietnam war than it does as these words are written.

Suppose now a bumper sticker that says "Make Love Not War." This requires us to bring something very concrete, the physical act of love, into opposition with something also phenomenal but less concrete. To make love is to do a very specific thing. To make war is to do any number of possible things not named specifically in this message. But the private context of lovemaking and public context of armed combat come together somehow in our minds, reinforced by the form of the message, in which the same verb governs two disparate nouns. This is a figure of speech, which the rhetoricians can name for us, but the point is that the figure unites two disparate contexts. Furthermore, the whole thing makes concrete that original abstraction, "peace," by turning it into the specific form of physical love.

I have seen a version of this sticker that adds a visual sign: two rhinoceroses copulating. This addition of another context compounds the wit, and the literariness, of the message. To show such obviously martial beasts performing their thunderous analogue to the lovemaking of human couples reminds us in a very complex way of our connection to and difference from other animals; it may remind us of the warrior Mars, in his armor, courting Venus; or it may cause us to wonder whether we humans have advanced as much over the other beasts in our capacity for love as we have in our military capability. All these reflections are an aspect of our literary competence as interpreters, to be sure, but they are encouraged by the text, which unites words and picture to point to so many relevant contexts in our semiotically coded cultural world. We might observe further here that the purely semiotic play of context makes the sticker more interesting in itself and less dependent on any particular sociopolitcal context than a simple "Peace" sign, which needs a war as context to fulfill its semiotic function.

Take another sticker that says "Make Love Not Babies." This is perhaps the most literary of all the stickers we have considered. It replaces some direct monocontextual sign such as "Zero Population Growth" or "Fight Overpopulation," and it makes these general and rather abstract notions concrete. But it also alludes in a purely semiotic way to the chronologically earlier sign, "Make Love Not War." That is, one context here is essentially semiotic—in this case verbal—while the other is essentially phenomenal, addressing the question of overpopulation. Once again, the sign maker has taken advantage of our English-speaking propensity to "make" everything under the sun, in order to let that verb govern two different subjects. But for those readers who know the earlier—"Make Love Not War"—sign, he has done something special; he has prepared a trap, a surprise of the sort Stanley Fish made famous in *Surprised by Sin* and *Self-Consuming Artifacts*. The antiwar reader and the pro-birth-control reader may not be the same person. And even if a person holds both these attitudes, the shift in the last word of the second sign from "War" to "Babies" comes as a shock. Where the first sign took love and war, those natural, almost binary, opposites, and juxtaposed them, this sign brings together eroticism and conception, which, after all, are intimately connected. The overpopulation problem, phenomenal to be sure, but generalized and almost abstract, is brought home to our very beds. And the statement invokes yet another context, the theological, which in our tradition has habitually insisted that procreation is the only justification for the act of love.

The reader possessing literary competence here may be led to invent the Church's countersign, a sticker that sternly advises us to "Make Babies Not Love." This, of course, would be ludicrous, since the Church professes to have nothing against lovemaking. The sign is not reversible, which is part of the point. It is perhaps fair to question whether I have been too competent an interpreter here, gone to too many contexts in reading this particular message.

This is a crucial point, and may serve to help situate semiotic interpretation among the other interpretive methods. I would suggest that this bumper sticker is, in its modest way, an example of what Umberto Eco calls an "open work" (see *The Role of the Reader*). Granting that it makes a rhetorical point on behalf of a particular ideology (which, if that were all, would make it a "closed" work), it also transcends this persuasive function by allowing for extensive interpretation that is guided, though not limited, by its verbal text. As semiotic interpreters we are not free to *make* meaning, but we are free to *find* it by following the various semantic, syntactic, and pragmatic paths that lead away from the words of the text. That is, we can't bring just any meanings to the text, but we can bring all the meanings we can link to the text by means of an interpretive code. And, above all, we can generate meaning by situating this text among the actual and possible texts to which it can be related.

Up to now, we have been considering the dynamics of literariness in minimal situations, just one level removed from ordinary discourse—acts of communication not usually regarded as literature. At this point it will be necessary to shift to the other end of the verbal spectrum—to codify briefly the major elements of literariness and to correlate them, if possible, with what are traditionally recognized as the major forms of literature. The following list should help tidy things up:

1. Duplicity of sender—role-playing, acting
2. Duplicity of receiver—eavesdropping, voyeurism
3. Duplicity of message—opacity, ambiguity
4. Duplicity of context—allusion, fiction
5. Duplicity of contact—translation, fiction
6. Duplicity of code—involved in all the above

The forms of discourse that we regularly recognize as literature—play, poem, and story—are dominated by the conventions listed here. The theater is an arena specifically structured to facilitate role-playing by actors and eavesdropping/voyeurism by spectators. The poem is dominated by sound effects and verbal strategies that stimulate our awareness of the message as a specific, unique thing. And the story is a description of situations and a narration of actions that are not present to us but are totally created by the discourse, requiring us to visualize and respond emotionally to events we cannot enter as persons, though we may well connect them to our personal experiences.

This point can stand some elaboration, since it touches again on the key question of how semiotic systems may or may not be connected to the phenomenal or experiential world. The argument being presented here is that one context, made out of perceptual and experiential data held in common by author and audience, is always invoked by any fictional or mimetic context, whether "realistic" or "fantastic." This "real" context provides a background against which we perceive and measure any pseudo-experiential or fictional context presented to us. At this point we must consider the view that the "real" context is also a fiction, since it is based on past experience, no longer directly available. This view is partly true. Our memories of experience must be differentiated from the experience itself. But so must our memories of actual experience be differentiated from any ideas we may acquire about things we have never experienced through our own perceptions. As memory grows fainter the events remembered lose their reality. But it is not until we try to reconstruct these fading events that fiction is generated. The passage of real experience into the past is not itself fictional, but all attempts to reconstruct are precisely that: fictions. Fiction is not what is lost but what is constructed. Our memories are of events we once had access to as persons, with power to influence them by our presence at the time when they occurred. But in the pseudo-experiential context of constructed events we are not present as persons—ever.

We may watch a performance of *Hamlet* but we cannot enter it or alter it as fiction in any way. We can disturb the actors but we cannot influence the characters, for whom we are less real than Hamlet's father or the king's jester Yorick. The painted peach we cannot eat, the flowers we cannot smell, the dreadful deed we can do nothing to prevent, these are the signs of fiction or illusion, that concrete world in which we are no more than ghostly observers. The world created by a fiction, then, whether a story, play, or poem, is one context we perceive and half create around the message that directs our thoughts. But behind that world or around it is our own phenomenal world, in which the fictional events reverberate. What we know from experience of love and lust, charity and hate, pleasure and pain, we bring to bear upon the fictional events—inevitably, because we seek to make every text our own. And what we find in fiction leaks out to color our phenomenal world, to help us assign meaning, value, and importance to the individual events and situations of our lives.

Many fictions, of course, insist that their context is not fictional at all, that they speak directly to us of the things around us. Others insist that their context is of imagination all compact, that in their fictional worlds is no contamination from our own. Both, of course, are wrong. Our world, our life, the knowledge we have of what our senses have allowed us to perceive, is with us always, and we know analogues in our own experience for the fairest damsels, the cruelest ogres, and the bravest heroes of all fairyland. Much of literary competence is based upon our ability to connect the worlds of fiction and experience. And much of our literature quite rightly insists upon that very connection.

When a writer allows his book to be called *Winesburg, Ohio*, for instance, his title names both a fictional town and a real state, telling us that this is fiction, yes, but that it has a real context as well.

When a writer calls his book *Dubliners*, and situates the fictional names of his characters among the real names of his city, he is asking us to use the fiction not as some pure artifact but as information about the way real people behave in a real place. And we must not see this as a regrettable impurity in otherwise beautiful art: we must see it as a strong assertion of the cognitive function of literature, which is an essential part of it. The real context is always present; the fictional one does not efface it but brings some aspects of it into a particular focus for our scrutiny. All fairy tales tell us something about reality.

Both plays and stories generate fictional contexts, as I have been suggesting, but a performance or enactment (whether of a play proper or of a story dramatized for the occasion) alters the way in which a fictional context is generated. (So too, of course, does cinema; but the coding of fictional films will require separate treatment.) Dramatization by actors of fictional situations reduces the need for fictionalizing by a single interpreter or reader, since it transfers some of the interpretive burden to director and actors, while it allows each spectator to submerge his or her individual interpretive identity in the collective reaction of an audience. The burden of literariness in live theater is divided among a number of aspects of communication, but it is dominated by the situation of enactment itself.

Poems, too, can be enacted, and they certainly generate fictional contexts, but the dominant feature of poetical composition is surely to be found at the level of the message itself, where versification, figuration, and other linguistic strategies make themselves felt. And just as poems are frequently fictional, plays and stories regularly use the linguistic resources of poetry. And all three of these forms regularly enrich their contextual reference by pointing toward other communicative acts, by quoting, alluding, parodying, and otherwise generating a context that is entirely semiotic and intertextual. Major literary works are all comments on their own form, on the generic tradition or traditions from which they take their being. The study of literature, then, must involve the study of communicative process in general—or semiotics—and in particular the development of the codes that govern the production and interpretation of the major kinds of literature, and the subcodes that inform the various genres that have developed in the course of literary history.

As I have been suggesting, the forms we recognize most readily as literary—play, poem, and story—though given to exploiting the communicative resources that determine their particular codes and qualities, also borrow freely from the coding of the other forms. Each "form" is only a codification of certain communicative procedures that have proved effective through time. It is also true that forms less obviously literary often turn to the codes of literature for their own purposes. The essay, for instance, frequently occasions debate as to its status. Are essays literature or are they not? The answer, it seems to me, is simple. Essays are not necessarily literary but become so to the extent that they adopt the dominant qualities of any of the three major forms of literature. The more an essay alludes or fictionalizes, the more the author adopts a role or suggests one for the reader, the more the language becomes sonorous or figured, the more literary the essay (or the letter, the prayer, the speech, etc.) becomes.

Finally, it should be made clear that literariness in itself ought not to be confused with value. All plays are literary but all are not equally valuable. And our reasons for valuing a play may have as much to do with its function as with its form. To the extent that a work of literature points toward our experience as living human beings, we may value it for what we call its "truth" or "rightness"—which is not a specifically formal quality but a matter of the fit between a message and its existential context. This opens up an area for discussion too large to be considered here. Suffice it to note that literary coding of discourse is a formal strategy, a means of structuring that enables the maker of the discourse to communicate certain kinds of meaning. We may, of course, value some literary utterances mainly for their formal elegance, but we also may value literary utterances for the insight they provide about aspects of existence, and it would be foolish to pretend this is not so simply because it does not lend itself to formal codification.

This means, of course, that the student and teacher of literary texts will have to be something of a historian and something of a philosopher if he or she wishes to approach full understanding of the texts—and even something of a person. Many literary works assume experience of life as an aspect of their context shared by writer and reader. Some works refuse to open to us until we are sufficiently mature. Others close as we lose access to some contexts through growing or forgetting. No study of literature can be purely formal, and all attempts to reduce literary study to this level are misguided, if not pernicious. To the extent that semiotic studies insist that communication is a matter of purely formal systems, they too may be misguided if not pernicious. Many semioticians would argue that the meaning of any sign or word is purely a function of its place in a paradigmatic system and its use in a syntagmatic situation. But I wish to suggest that meaning is also a function of human experience. For those who have experienced such things as marriage or bereavement the words themselves will signify something different than they will for those who have had no experience of these things—and much of literature is based on attempts to generate semiotic equivalents for experiences that seem to defy duplication in mere signs.

Having uttered this necessary corrective to extreme versions of formalist and structuralist theory, I must conclude by reaffirming my own position as a student of literary semiotics. My whole argument here has been an attempt to show how the formal qualities of literature are the result of a process that multiplies or complicates the normal features of human communication. This activity must be based upon the pleasure inherent in the semiotic processes themselves—in their ability to generate and communicate meaning—which is an indispensable aspect of human existence. The imposition of additional forms of coding upon language to generate literary texts has a powerful element of play or game in it—but so does much of human acculturation. Going beyond the necessary is as typical of science as it is of art. The skills involved in making and interpreting the most complex literary structures presently being produced in our culture are of a high order, and they require training beyond mere linguistic competence for their development. The function of a semiotics of literature lies in its ability to clarify this training and help to focus it on the communicative skills required to complete it. The value of such literary training to our whole culture lies in the ways that people trained in the semiotic subtleties of literary study may themselves use our communicative media to generate the ideas we need to keep that culture alive and functioning in a time which is certain to bring us to the point of crisis.

3

SEMIOTICS OF THE POETIC TEXT

Let us begin with one of the shortest poetic texts in the English language, "Elegy" by W. S. Merwin:

ELEGY
Who would I show it to

One line, one sentence, unpunctuated, but proclaimed an interrogative by its grammar and syntax—what makes it a poem? Certainly without its title it would not be a poem; but neither would the title alone constitute a poetic text. Nor do the two together simply make a poem by themselves. Given the title and the text, the *reader* is encouraged to make a poem. He is not forced to do so, but there is not much else he can do with this material, and certainly nothing else so rewarding. (I will use the masculine pronoun here to refer to the reader, not because all readers are male but because I am, and my hypothetical reader is not a pure construct but an idealized version of myself.)

How do we make a poem out of this text? There are only two things to work on, the title and the question posed by the single, colloquial line. The line is not simply colloquial, it is prosaic; with no words of more than one syllable, concluded by a preposition, it is within the utterance range of every speaker of English. It is, in a sense, completely intelligible. But in another sense it is opaque, mysterious. Its three pronouns—who, I, it—pose problems of reference. Its conditional verb phrase—would...show to—poses a problem of situation. The context that would supply the information required to make that simple sentence meaningful as well as intelligible is not there. It must be supplied by the reader.

To make a poem of this text the reader must not only know English, he must know a poetic code as well: the code of the funeral elegy, as practiced in English from the Renaissance to the present time. The "words on the page" do not constitute a poetic "work," complete and self-sufficient, but a "text," a sketch or outline that must be completed by the active participation of a reader equipped with the right sort of information. In this case part of that information consists of an acquaintance with the elegiac tradition: its procedures, assumptions, devices, and values. One needs to know works like Milton's "Lycidas," Shelley's "Adonais," Tennyson's "In Memoriam," Whitman's "When Lilacs Last in the Dooryard Bloomed," Thomas's "Refusal to Mourn the Death by Fire of a Child in London," and so on, in order to "read" this simple poem properly. In fact, it could be argued that the more elegies one can bring to bear on a reading of this one, the better, richer poem this one becomes. I would go even further, suggesting that a knowledge of the critical tradition—of Dr. Johnson's objections to "Lycidas," for instance, or Wordsworth's critique of poetic diction—will also enhance one's reading of this poem. For the poem is, of course, an anti-elegy, a refusal not simply to mourn, but to write a sonorous, eloquent, mournful, but finally acquiescent, accepting—in a word, "elegiac"—poem at all.

Reading the poem involves, then, a special knowledge of its tradition. It also involves a special interpretive skill. The forms of the short, written poem as they have developed in English over the past few centuries can be usefully seen as compressed, truncated, or fragmented imitations of other verbal forms, especially the play, story, public oration, and personal essay. The reasons for this are too complicated for consideration here, but the fact will be apparent to all who reflect upon the matter. Our short poems are almost always elliptical version of what can easily be conceived of as dramatic, narrative, oratorical, or meditative texts. Often, they are combinations of these and other modes of address. To take an obvious example, the dramatic monologue in the hands of Robert Browning is like a speech from a play (though usually more elongated than most such speeches). But to "read" such a monologue we must imagine the setting, the situation, the context, and so on. The dramatic monologue is "like" a play but gives us less information of certain sorts than a play would, requiring us to provide that information by decoding the clues in the monologue itself in the light of our understanding of the generic model. Most short poems work this way. They require both special knowledge and special skills to be "read."

To understand "Elegy" we must construct a situation out of the clues provided. The "it" in "Who would I show it to" is of course the elegy itself. The "I" is the potential writer of the elegy. The "Who" is the audience for the poem. But the verb phrase "would...show to" indicates a condition contrary to fact. Who would I show it to *if* I were to write it? This implies in turn that for the potential elegiac poet there is one person whose appreciation means more than that of all the rest of the potential audience for the poem he might write, and it further implies that the death of this particular person is the one imagined in the poem. If this person were dead, the poet suggests, so would his inspiration be dead. With no one to write for, no poem would be forthcoming. This poem is not only a "refusal to mourn," like that of Dylan Thomas, it is a refusal to elegize. The whole elegiac tradition, like its cousin the funeral oration, turns finally away from mourning toward acceptance, revival, renewal, a return to the concerns of life, symbolized by the very writing of the poem. Life goes on; there *is* an audience; and the mourned person will live through accomplishments, influence, descendants, and also (not least) in the elegiac poem itself. Merwin rejects all that. *If* I wrote an elegy for X, the person for whom I have always written, X would not be alive to read it; therefore, there is no reason to write an elegy for the one person in my life who most deserves one; therefore, there is no reason to write any elegy, anymore, ever. Finally, and of course, this poem called "Elegy" is not an elegy.

Am I pushing my interpretation too far? If you go in the right direction, there is no such thing as too far. All the elegies ever written will enrich our understanding of this poem. And all the ramifications of situation that can be developed from the hints in this one line are also relevant. On any line of interpretation one will reach a point of diminishing returns, but the zero point is infinitely far away. Considered semiotically, the important aspects of this little interpretive exercise are these: (1) to read the poem we must know its generic tradition (what Gérard Genette has called "the architext"—see *L'introduction à l'architexte* [Seuil, 1979]) and a certain number of the texts in that tradition; and (2) we must have some skill at supplying the elements (narrative, dramatic, oratorical, personal) that are lacking because of the elliptical nature of poetic utterance. Combined, these indicate the major premise of any semiotic study of poetry: that a poem is a text connected to other texts, requiring the active participation of a skilled reader for its interpretation.

The other texts need not be parts of a tradition sanctioned by "high" culture; they may just as easily be taken from popular tradition, as another short poem by Merwin will show. It is called "When the War is Over":

> When the war is over
> We will be proud of course the air will be
> Good for breathing at last
> The water will have been improved the salmon
> And the silence of heaven will migrate more perfectly
> The dead will think the living are worth it we will know
> Who we are
> And we will all enlist again

This is a poem of the 1960s, and one could gloss it by reference to the Vietnam war, but that is hardly a necessary feature of its interpretation. Much more important in the way of information is a folk ditty sung in many wars by soldiers and sailors (I have sung it myself in ports from Newport, R. I. to Yokosuka, Japan during the Korean "police action") in anticipation of their release from military duties. It is sung to the stirring tune of "The Battle Hymn of the Republic," beginning with "When the war is over we will all enlist again" repeated several times, and concluding with a variety of expletivious lines, ranging from "We will, like hell we will" to "In a pig's asshole we will." The folk song is based on a simple ironic reversal—we *will* enlist again is maintained until the last line, where that sentiment is firmly rejected.

Merwin has re-reversed the sentiment of the folk song, saying, in effect, we think we won't enlist again, but, fatally, we will, we will. Formally, he has done this by taking the first line of the folk song— "When the war is over we will all enlist again"—and spreading it out. "When the war is over" becomes the first line of his poem and "we will all enlist again" becomes the last. In between is the material that makes this text a poem, for the reader who has the equipment to read it. For our purposes this material can also serve to illustrate some of the principles of poetic discourse formulated by Michael Riffaterre in his *Semiotics of Poetry*. The way this poem grows out of the folk song by its negation or inversion is one of the typical features of poetic discourse. Texts emerge from other "intertexts" or from matrices provided by discursive tradition. Merwin's development of his material is also quintessentially poetic by Riffaterre's criteria, which, to a considerable extent, I accept. What Merwin does with the central material of the poem is to move gradually from the prosaic to the poetic, before falling back to the prosaic for the last line, which is now transfigured by the preceding material. Let us look more carefully at how this works. "When the war is over/We will be proud of course...." This is a perfectly prosaic sentence; that is, it poses no problems in grammar, syntax, or semantics for the reader (except that the reader himself must close the sentence by mentally inserting the period in the right place). The reader's sense of grammar is not allowed to operate passively but must take an active hand in constructing the poem from the text. Still, the grammatical clues are so straightforward that this gesture of sentence closure is not difficult to make.

There is only one tiny problem. The sentence could be closed after "proud," and the phrase "of course" can either end the first sentence or begin the second. This is not important, but it is a warning of more significant "ungrammaticalities" to come. There are other traps or invitations to stretch the limits of grammatical and semantic coding as we proceed. Since the text lacks all conventional marks of prosaic punctuation, the conventions of poetic punctuation loom larger. The lines begin with capital letters and end with space. Each line is a discrete unit, something like a sentence. Thus, though we can find a prosaic place for a period in the middle of some lines, we are led toward a different mode of reading as well, with the elements of each line functioning as a grammatical unit. If we take "We will be proud of course the air will be" as a strong syntactical unit, a complete sentence, the parallelism of "we will be" and "the air will be" draws both these auxiliary phrases toward the yoke (or zeugma, in rhetorical parlance) of the predicate adjective, "proud." The air will be proud? Impossible! Surely the poet wouldn't want us to think that. I wouldn't be too sure. Roman Jakobson has cogently argued that parallelism of various sorts is the major feature of poetic grammar. That potential zeugma, with its semantic absurdity, haunts the second line of the poem without insisting that we attend to it. Further on, there will be anomalies too palpable to be ignored.

At this point, however, the text allows us to make a second sentence easily, coming to a full stop comfortably at the end of line 3: "the air will be/Good for breathing at last." The only problem here is the slight semantic strain involved in finding a causal reason for the connection between the improvement in the air and the end of the war. This amounts to a threat against what Riffaterre calls "mimesis"—that is, our ability to assign referential status to the things apparently designated by the text. If we understand that the air will be "literally," as we say, improved, then we are reading the word "air" mimetically. If, on the other hand, we take the word, as we say, figuratively, then we have been driven from a mimetic reading to what Riffaterre calls a "semiotic" one. This frustration of mimesis by semantic impossibility is a regular feature of poetic texts. In the present case, such familiar figures as "to breathe easier" inhabit the same semantic space as "the air will be good for breathing," but the poet has unpacked the domesticated version and allowed the strangeness of the image to become perceptible again. Still, interpretation continues to be easy; the strangeness is perceived as a kind of noise, not as a message in another code.

With the fourth line the strangeness of poetic speech is fully upon us: "The water will have been improved the salmon." The move from air to water is natural. They are elemental substances, frequently associated in poetic discourse. But the causal relationship between the end of the war and the improvement in air can hardly be stretched to water. One may say, oh, well, after the war even the water will taste better. Perhaps, but there are salmon in this water and they will not go away.

A part of every reader of poetry must be a reader of prose. The effort of making a poem from a poetic text requires the increase of energy caused by frustration of prosaic interpretation. If the reader doesn't strain after prose sense, poetic readings will hardly be attained. The skill required for poetic interpretation involves a strong concern for prosaic meaning combined with a readiness to push beyond the prosaic to generate new meanings. In semiotic terms this often means that the established codes of interpretation, whether grammatical or lexical, may have to be reconstructed. This is work, productive labor. Its immediate reward is the satisfaction of interpretation itself, making a poem from the text, but there are other and perhaps greater rewards for the individual interpreter, in the forms of gains in flexibility and verbal skill, along with possession of enriched semantic and syntactic codes.

Returning to the poem, the interpreter must deal with the salmon. They have appeared "naturally" in the water by a familiar process of association: metonymy. But grammatically and logically (causally) they are not easy to fit into the picture. If the line is to be read as a whole and complete sentence, the salmon will have to be read as "improved" along with the water. This is not merely difficult mimetically but virtually impossible. The sensitive interpreter begins at this point to wonder whether impossibility itself may not be presiding over the poem. Improved air is close enough to already coded metaphors that have died and become clichés, so that we breathe easily enough in our interpretation of that metaphor. But improved salmon must give us considerable pause. Perhaps we can solve our problem by inserting a period before the salmon, so that they may leap into the next sentence, where they will indeed go naturally with the verb "migrate," making an old familiar combination. Salmon and migration go together like sardines and crowdedness. We take comfort from these regular associations.

But poetic texts are designed to discomfort us first of all. Any comfort we get from them must be earned. "The salmon and the silence of heaven will migrate more perfectly"—there is our new next sentence and it works fine syntactically. What Riffaterre would call its "ungrammaticality" comes at the level of semantics and mimesis, not at the level of grammar as such. Yes, the salmon will migrate after the war, as they have doubtless migrated all through it, since they must; they are genetically programmed to do so. But their migration is a part of the order of things on this earth and can scarcely be improved. And the "silence of heaven" is by any definition beyond such timebound, earthbound things as migration and improvement. No, it has not improved, nor will it migrate. Following the poet along his metonymic trail we have come up against a wall of negation, a cosmic irony. The disruption of mimesis is absolute, leading us to read some level of ironic denial into all the poem's assertions. The textual utterance about the migration of the heavenly silence is the poetic counterpart of the folk song's utterance about the pig's asshole. They are, in their different ways, contradictions sufficiently powerful to direct all interpreters toward the ironic mode of reading.

In "The dead will think the living are worth it" and "we will know / Who we are" the text offers us two statements that are simple grammatically but complex semantically and fraught with ironies. Then comes the "And," the innocent copula, which alerts us to the poem's impending closure, and joins this statement to all the others. But where the others are qualified or negated by irony, this one is perfectly straightforward, though dripping, now, with the sarcasm that flows from the preceding ironies. We *will* all enlist again, as surely as the salmon migrate—and *that* is who we are. We need not literally enlist; the whole poem is an extended metaphor, an allegory of an aspect of human nature that is despicable: that we enlist again and again in destructive enterprises, caring not enough about the air, the water, the living creatures, the dead, the earth, the heavens. And here is where I part company with Michael Riffaterre. Where he is content to point out how poetic texts cut themselves off from direct mimetic or referential connection to reality, I would insist that in many cases, perhaps most, they circle back allegorically to reference once again. That is, we, the readers, the interpreters, bring them back by going through them, to their ends.

This question of the relationship between the poetic text and the world is simply a special case of the larger debate over the relationship between all linguistic utterances and the world, or, put most brutally, between words and things. Without attempting to resolve the dispute, or even to argue a case very strongly, I should like to situate the semiotic interpretation of poetry in relation to the larger question. This work of situation has already been performed by Paul Ricoeur, in his important study, translated as *The Rule of Metaphor* (Toronto, 1977), but it has been performed in a most disingenuous and misleading way, which will require some serious examination.

In his third chapter, "Metaphor and the Semantics of Discourse," Ricoeur proposes to us a "distinction between semiotics and semantics," which he attributes to the French structural linguist Emile Benveniste. Ricoeur then proceeds to quote from several pages of Benveniste's *Problems in General Linguistics*, in which Benveniste discusses the levels of linguistic analysis from the word to the sentence to the largest unit—discourse. We may note two things about Benveniste's actual discussion (pp. 101–11). First, he *never* makes any distinction there between semiotics and semantics; and second, he never considers at all, in any way, the relationship between language and the world. His essential distinction is between "language as a system of signs" and "language as an instrument of communication," which is simply a restatement of Saussure's distinction between *langue* and *parole*, language and speech. For Benveniste, meaning in language as a whole is systematic; meaning in speech or utterance is situational. In terms of the most elementary distinctions in semiotic studies, meaning in language as a system is semantic; in the single sentence meaning is modified by syntactic meaning; and in speech or discourse the other forms of meaning are further shaped by pragmatics: the relations between the speakers and the situation of their discourse.

This is simple enough, but Ricoeur translates it into the following invidious distinction, in which he has implicated Benveniste: "Semiotics is aware only of intra-linguistic relationships, whereas semantics takes up the relationship between the sign and the things denoted—that is, ultimately, the relationship between language and the world" (p. 74). Unfortunately, Ricoeur himself, Benveniste, and a horde of others have been busy showing that there is no "relationship" between *language* and the world. Reference to the world is not fixed in language. It is a fluctuating function of speech, of utterance, of human communication. Ricoeur has not only reified—or rather, personified—such abstractions as semiotics and semantics, he has forgotten his own point about the difference between words and propositions. In his system words do not refer to things but propositions or sentences do. In Benveniste's

view, however, sentences do not have meaning by virtue of reference but because they are parts of larger discursive structures.
They are meaningful in a specific discursive situation, and their
"reference" is to that situation only. He offers us no easy jump
from word to world.

I have considered this at length—and perhaps with some heat—
because it *is* an important issue that is not helped by such distinctions as the one Ricoeur makes between semiotics and semantics.
Reference, in fact, is still a very live issue among semioticians. In
our particular concern here, the semiotics of poetry, we should
remember that Jakobson never excluded the referential function
from poetic utterance; he only said that it was not dominant in
poetry and that it was often complicated by ambiguity. Michael
Riffaterre has taken up Ricoeur's gauntlet and argued that poetry *is*
essentially antimimetic and nonreferential. But Yuri Lotman, the
most interesting of the current generation of Soviet semioticians,
has argued what seems to be the opposite side of the case. Lotman's view of poetry, as articulated in *Analysis of the Poetic Text*,
is clear, powerful, and worth considering in some detail.

Lotman, in fact, sets poetic discourse against three kinds of "automism," and he means by automism something very like I. A.
Richards's notion of "stock response." These are: (1) the automism of language, (2) the automism of "common sense," and (3)
the automism of our "spatio-visual" picture of the world. Against
the inertia of these three systems—habitual modes of perception,
of thought, and of speech—the poet and the poem go to work. Let
me illustrate with another simple poem by W. S. Merwin:

> Separation
> Your absence has gone through me
> Like thread through a needle.
> Everything I do is stitched with its color.

This simple poem is complex in Lotman's sense because it violates
expectations in all three of his frameworks, and poetic information, like any other kind of information, is inversely proportional to
its expectedness. The first line seems to start us along the syntactic
road of a familiar cliché: "gone through me like a knife"; or a needle or some other sharp instrument. The poem then violates our

expectation by grasping the unexpected end of the needle. Our common sense tells us that separation is painful. We expect an image to be presented that will concentrate on pain—something that a needle could easily accomplish. But instead the image presented focuses our attention on the ubiquity of the feeling of separation rather than its acuteness. Finally, our spatial-visual sense tells us that a person cannot be visualized as a kind of needle going around stitching things with a thread the color of absence. We cannot, on this level, even say what color the thread is. It *won't* visualize. But this unvisualizable "image" carries its meaning with the kind of vigor that only poetry can command. To comprehend the image we must move to a higher level of abstraction, where its significance emerges as a concept—pervasiveness, ubiquity, or inevitability—but a concept energized by our movement from the image to the theme it signifies. We might add that the apparent "ordinariness" of the language of the poem may itself be seen as a violation of "poetic" expectations. As Lotman points out, "not only the retreat from the natural norms of language but also their approximation can be a source of artistic effect" (p. 133).

It should be clear that Lotman's view of poetry is in many respects similar to Riffaterre's. They both stress the deviance or ungrammaticality of the poetic text and the need for the reader to actively make meaning, recoding his language and cultural framework as necessary. But they appear to differ profoundly on the question of reference. Let me bring this difference to a sharper focus. Riffaterre says, everywhere and often, what we can find him saying of a Victor Hugo poem in "Une lecture de Hugo" from *La Production du texte* (Seuil, 1979): "La comparaison du poème avec la réalité est une approche critique d'efficacité douteuse" (p. 176). Lotman says, in no uncertain terms, something that appears completely contradictory:

> The aim of poetry, of course, is not "devices" but a knowledge of the world and the relationship among people, self-knowledge, and the development of the human personality in the process of learning and social communication. In the final summing up, the goal of poetry coincides with the goal of culture as a whole. But poetry realizes this goal specifically, and an understanding of its specific character is impossible if one ignores its mechanism, its internal structure. This

mechanism actually is more readily revealed when it enters into conflict with the automism of language. [pp. 132–33]

Behind Riffaterre, Mallarmé; behind Lotman, Viktor Shklovsky's insistence that "art exists to help us recover the sensation of life; it exists to make us feel things, to make the stone *stony*." Both Lotman and Riffaterre are semioticians, but one writes out of a French tradition, the other out of a Slavic one. Even so, I wish to argue that they are not so far apart as they seem. They both note that poetic texts challenge our accepted modes of speech, perception, and belief. But where Lotman believes that such challenges bring us dialectically to a greater understanding of the world, Riffaterre is silent, skeptical. Let us say, then, that within semiotic studies the question is open, unsettled. You know where I stand.

There is one other important difference between Lotman and Riffaterre that we should consider before closing this brief incursion into the semiotics of poetry. Riffaterre not only emphasizes the process whereby texts grow out of previous texts, he makes it the exclusive form of poetic genesis. There is something hyperbolical and, well, French about this that I admire and distrust—but he is terribly persuasive as a reader of poetic texts. Lotman does not take up the subject of poetic genesis so directly, but he seems to feel that poems can come from almost anywhere, so long as they adopt the techniques that will enable us to recognize and read them as poetry. In the examples used so far, it has been apparent that the short poems of W. S. Merwin respond to both sorts of semiotic reading. I chose poems by Merwin because I admire them, because they are short, and because they are in the mainstream of English poetry. But it might be argued that this makes them too poetical, too open to the sort of semiotic reading I have proposed. Let me close, then, with two poems of a different sort—in the American grain—that are perhaps less obvious in presenting themselves as poetic texts. First, a short poem by William Carlos Williams called "Nantucket":

Flowers through the window
lavender and yellow

changed by white curtains—
Smell of cleanliness—

Sunshine of a late afternoon—
On the glass tray
a glass pitcher, the tumbler
turned down, by which
a key is lying—And the
immaculate white bed

This poem names a real place, Nantucket Island, Mas-
sachusetts, in its title. But it is also a literary place in the American
tradition. Here Ishmael signed on the *Pequod* for the voyage he
narrates in *Moby Dick*. The island boasts a whaling museum, a
harbor, beaches, seabirds, and one of the loveliest old towns in the
United States. The poet evokes this cultural heritage by naming the
island in his title, but the poetic text offers us none of these things.
It presents another image of Nantucket, no less real, perhaps, but
made more intense because of its distance from the more automatic
connotations of the name.

This is one sort of "ungrammaticality"—a mild surprise that we
shall reconsider later on, after looking at the surprises—also
mild—in prosaic and poetic grammar. The poetic convention of
starting all lines with capitalization is violated in this poem. The
capitalization appears erratic, in fact, until we realize it is prosaic.
The poem consists of five T-units, as the new grammarians used to
say, that is, five independent clauses that might be punctuated as
separate sentences or as parts of one long, compound sentence.
The text actually has it both ways: each of these five units begins
with a capital letter, as if it were a sentence, but they are divided
not by periods but by dashes—internal marks of sentence punctuation. The five units, and the poem as a whole, lack main verbs as
well, so that the entire poem is, according to prose grammar, a
fragment. Still, it is a very complete poem. We adjust easily to
these mild ungrammaticalities, especially if we recognize the
poem's roots in the imagist tradition. To actually make a poem out
of this text, however, we shall have to accomplish three things. We
shall have to construct for it a complete discursive syntax, a
semantic pattern, and a pragmatic situation.

Let us begin with the situation. Where are we, and how do we
know? On Nantucket, of course, but where? The clues in the poem
make it clear that we are indoors, in a room. The flowers are out-

side, seen through a window, "changed by white curtains." The "smell of cleanliness" is an indoor smell, a human product. The sunlight is coming into the room. The room contains a bed and a glass tray in addition to the curtains. It is a bedroom. The pitcher and tumbler suggest that it is a guest room. The whole movement of eye from window to bed, and the sort of detail noticed, suggest that it is an unfamiliar room. (We do not smell our own room's odor, whether cleanly or not.) Finally, the key suggests that this is a rented room, a room in a "guest house" on Nantucket, for only in such a room is one likely to find that combination of pitcher, glass, bed, and key. Our interpretation of the clues depends upon some combination of cultural knowledge and experience. Using this information, we have constructed a pragmatics for the poem from the text, realizing a human situation. We are seeing, smelling, *noticing* an unfamiliar room, perhaps in a paid guest house. But this is about as far as we can go with the situation. What of the poem's semantic structure?

Semantic structure is something the reader achieves by sorting through the connotations of the words and phrases of the text, looking for patterns. It takes no great effort to see that this poem offers us in its opening lines three colors—lavender, yellow, and white—and that of the three it is white that dominates, being repeated in the last line of the text. White is also tied by association of ideas and values (a familiar sort of metonymy) to the two crucial, valorizing words in the poem: "cleanliness" and "immaculate." These connotations and these values dominate the poem. This is not the Nantucket of Ahab and Ishmael, redolent of the blood and blubber of sperm whales. This is the Nantucket of the Quaker ladies who stayed home. The bed and the key, peace and privacy; white curtains, white bed, glass pitcher and tumbler, purity. That is the connotative or semantic structure of the poem: a simple process of valorizing the Quaker heritage in the concrete details of a guest room democratically open to all. The key makes this sanctuary any person's castle while he or she inhabits it.

The text also encourages us to construct a syntactic pattern. There is coordinated movement here, along several lines. Though all but pastel colors are excluded, there is a movement from the darkest, lavender, to yellow, to a lavender and yellow "changed" (veiled, softened) by white, to the whitest of whites, immaculate. There is also a movement, of the eye at least, from outdoors—through the window, to noticing the outdoors come inside—the sunshine—to indoor things, pitcher and tumbler, to the innermost, secret indoor things, the key and the bed. The text seems to a casual glance to offer us an almost random collection of details from outdoors and inside, but attention to this ordering, to the semantic connotations of these details, and to the pragmatics of the situation, enables us to perceive a poem with a high degree of necessity in its choice and arrangement of visual detail. The valorizing word "immaculate" closes the value system of the poem, taking a step in intensity beyond mere cleanliness; the repetition of the color "white" closes the color system firmly; and the naming of the last object in the room, "bed," brings both eye and thought firmly to rest. Williams once said he did not think a poem should click like a box, but he certainly knew how to bring one to an end when it seemed appropriate.

We can receive a text like this lazily, consuming it as a vague impression, or we can take an active part in constructing its meanings, exploring its syntactic, semantic, and pragmatic coding, semiotically. If we do this, as we have done it here, we will see how Williams, in his mild way, does violate our automatic expectations with respect to grammar and punctuation, with regard, also, to our "common-sense" cultural knowledge of Nantucket, and that he allows us to be disoriented in space until we find the key to the poetic situation he has constructed. By following these active, analytic procedures in our reading, I would argue, we experience more pleasure from our encounter with the poetic text, we appreciate the poet's work more thoroughly, and we can take a certain amount of pride in sharing in the labor that made the poem from the text. Our reading has shown this apparently casual and impressionistic poem to have a high degree of what Riffaterre calls "monumentality," by which he means a necessity in the selection and ordering of its words, calculated to give them a durability, a necessity that links the poetic text and the codes required to interpret it, in a complex communicative net. This is the essential quality of poetry, and we can find it in every text that facilitates our effort to construct from it a poem.

I will conclude this discussion of the semiotics of poetry by looking at a text that appears initially to be almost entirely prosaic. It
resembles an entry in a diary or journal, apparently referring directly to a real experience, uniquely that of the person who wrote it
down, Gary Snyder:

All through the rains
That mare stood in the field—
A big pine tree and a shed,
But she stayed in the open
Ass to the wind, splash wet.
I tried to catch her April
For a bareback ride,
She kicked and bolted
Later grazing fresh shoots
In the shade of the down
Eucalyptus on the hill.

In selecting the poems to be considered in this chapter, I have
avoided all older poems and all poems with pronounced metrical
structures or formal rhyme schemes. Semiotic critics like Jakobson have shown many times over the extraordinary sound structures that work in traditional verse in a wide variety of languages. I
have chosen modern and contemporary poetry precisely because it
is closer to prose, forcing us to consider poeticity primarily as an
aspect of sense rather than sound. Merwin, of course, frequently
uses a language rich in metaphoric and metonymic figures, thus
drawing his texts away from the prosaic. But Williams's "Nantucket" is virtually without metaphor and simile, deriving its poeticity
only from the systems of syntactic, semantic, and pragmatic progression that we have just considered. This text of Gary Snyder's,
however, seems to lack even that kind of implicit structure. Written out as prose, "All through the rains" would give few clues to its
possible status as a poem. Its actual ungrammaticalities (missing
words, run-on sentence) are more like the results of hasty jotting in
a journal than like those obviously planned deviations from normal
grammar that signal poeticity. In Williams's "Nantucket," for instance, every independent clause lacks a main verb. Here, some
do, some do not. How can one read this text as a poem?

If a text offers too many difficulties to a semiotician approaching it as poetry, this obviously may be the result of either weakness in the approach or deficiencies in the text. We may simply have a poor reader, an inadequate methodology, or an unpoetic text. "All through the rains" in fact appears to be a borderline case—much less certainly within the domain of poetry than Snyder's "Riprap," for instance, or "Mid-August at Sourdough Mountain Lookout," from the same volume (*Riprap*, 1959). But let us see what we can do with it.

First of all, this text is related to others in the *Riprap* volume. It is in fact part of a sequence of poems from 1955 and 1956, a kind of poetic journal in which are recorded scenes, events, and thoughts leading up to and into Snyder's trip to the Far East, where he undertook a serious study of Buddhism and Oriental poetry. These texts compose a narrative of a man preparing himself for a major change of life. "All through the rains" is located between two longer poems of considerable strength. In the first, "Nooksack Valley," dated "February 1956," Snyder is watching a "huge setter pup" turning in circles and sleeping, while thinking about his own future, his plans to go back down the coast of California on Route 99, to San Francisco and Japan. The steelhead (trout) are running and he, too, will be on the move, "more.../Awake than ever before, yet ready to leave." What he is leaving is his whole twenty-five years of life: "damned memories,/Whole wasted theories, failures and worse success,/Schools, girls, deals." There are only three things I wish to say about this poem, which is too long to "read" here. First, it points very clearly to the larger, narrative structure, which is the structure of the poet's life, complete with dates, place names, and other specific references. Second, the poem is about the poet *as poet*, who speaks bitterly of his weakness in trying to make his own poems, including this one, too "poetic" in the bad, rhetorical sense: "To make this poem a froth, a pity." Third, the poetic technique the poet favors in contrast to the obviously manipulative figures of speech is the implied comparison or contrast between himself and something else that is before his eyes, especially something in nature. Like the steelhead, he will "run now" because it is time for him to do so. Unlike the dog, he will not turn and turn about, stop and sleep. These comparisons and contrasts are *not* explicit, which is one reason why they are poetical, but they are almost so, which is perhaps why they are not *very* poetical.

The poem that follows "All through the rain" is dated "April 1956" and bears the title "Migration of Birds," which is also the title of a book the poet is reading as he watches a hummingbird, listens to sparrows and a rooster, thinks about golden plover and the Arctic tern, notices the absence of juncos and robins. "Today that big abstraction's at our door," he writes, and closes the poem with thoughts of the seabirds across the hill, heading for Alaska. The next poem in the sequence is called "Tōji," and is located in Japan.

The poem we are looking at, then, is next to last in the sequence before the shift to Japan. This knowledge of the surrounding texts helps us to place this poem, to situate the "I" of it pragmatically in time, place, and disposition. Between February and April, this poem begins in March, with the rains, and moves into April in line 5. It is a fragmented narrative, made up of two incidents, both involving "that mare." Knowing that in the poetic code Snyder is developing for himself the implied comparison or contrast between human and animal is a principle discursive feature, we have a major clue for interpretation. In the two surrounding poems, Snyder has compared or contrasted himself, implicitly but somewhat obviously, to fish, birds, and, in the lines immediately before this poem, to a dog that "Turns and turns about, stops and sleeps." The parallel between man and mare in this poem is less obvious, more elliptical, and thus, if we can establish it, more poetical.

The text gives us two scenes, March and April, rainy and sunny. In the first the mare ignores the shelter offered by man (shed) and nature (pine tree) and just puts her ass to the wind, getting soaked. In the second, approached by man, in the person of the poet, seeking a ride, she is equally contrary. She resists nature (as rain) and culture (man, riding her as a "domesticated" animal) equally. In the rain she stays out; in the sun (and not the brutal sun of summer, but only an April sun on the north coast) she takes shelter. Contrariness, resistance, orneriness everywhere. It may seem that she gives in by sheltering under the fallen eucalyptus tree in the last lines, but this is precisely what she does not do, which makes this one of the most telling features in what proves to be an interesting and intricate little poem.

What is this "down/Eucalyptus," anyway? It is, first of all, a tree on a hill that has fallen down, but it is still providing shade. The text tells us all this. But it tells us nothing of the nature of the eucalyptus tree. This knowledge must come from elsewhere, and it is not likely to come simply from nature but from nature methodized—in a word, from a tree book, like "The Flower book and the Bird book and the Star book" that Snyder describes himself reading in "Things to Do Around a Lookout." I had seen (and smelled) eucalyptus trees for years, but it took a physicist and science fiction writer (Gregory Benford) to acquaint me with their history and characteristics. They are not native to this continent, but were imported from across the Pacific for lumber. They proved valueless, however, except for railroad ties, because their trunks and branches are too twisted to be sawed effectively. Unlike all other trees with leaves and bark, the eucalyptus keeps the leaves and sheds the bark, giving off a unique, pungent smell all the while. A most contrary tree.

When the mare that will not be ridden and the transplanted tree that will not be worked come together at the end of the poem, with the "down" tree *up* on a hill, and still holding on to its leaves, we have a conclusion that is inescapably poetic because it brings "a big abstraction" to our door. As potential horseman, Snyder could not mount the mare bareback, but he did not try to bridle her. As poet, he sees the conjunction of mare and tree as rich in textual possibilities and full of meaning for himself; his own bridling at the world of "theories, failures, worse success,/Schools, girls, deals" is reflected in these "unnatural" natural creatures. True to his desire to avoid froth and pity, he leaves the comparison between mare and tree, and between both of them and himself, completely unexplicit. If there is to be a metaphor here, the reader must make it, by knowing some other texts and bringing some interpretive skill to bear upon this one.

Snyder's text does not force us to poeticity by violating mimesis. We are free to regard it as a fragment of experience—which it may well be. But we are also free to make a poem of it, encouraged by its shape, its elliptical quality, its position among Snyder's other texts. And when we search for its poetic structure, we find it: consistency of connotation leading to a code or theme, elaborated in a parallel structure of binary oppositions brought to closure in the single memorable image of the cantankerous mare under the untamable tree.

A semiotic approach to poetry is neither vastly different from other effective approaches nor foolproof as a method. What it offers, as I hope I have demonstrated, is a methodology that is explicit, consistent, and therefore pedagogically useful as a way of developing interpretive flexibility and sensitivity in students of literature. In dealing with poetic texts, wherein meaning is primarily implicit, there is surely an important role for an approach to interpretation that aims at making the syntactic, semantic, and pragmatic structures of meaning as explicit as can be.

4

NARRATION AND NARRATIVITY IN FILM AND FICTION

Let us assume that there is something called narrative that can exist apart from any particular method of narration or any particular narrative utterance, as we assume that there is something called the English language that exists apart from any particular form of discourse or any individual speech act in English. Narration is, first of all, a kind of human behavior. It is specifically a mimetic or representative behavior, through which human beings communicate certain kinds of message. The modes of narration may vary extraordinarily. (In passing, I should say that I am aware of our customary distinction between what is told and what is enacted, which leads us to oppose narrative representation to dramatic enactment. In this case, however I am using the word "narration" in its broadest sense to include both plays and stories, along with other forms of imitation.) A narrative, then, may be recounted orally, committed to writing, acted out by a group of actors or a single actor, presented in wordless pantomime, or represented as a sequence of visual images, with or without words, or as a cinematic flow of moving pictures, with or without sounds, speech, music, and written language.

All of these mimetic kinds of behavior have certain features in common that enable us to consider them together as narrative. First of all, they belong to a special class of symbolic activity which forces the interpreter to make a distinction between his own immediate situation and some other situation that is being presented to him through the medium of narration. In narrative there is always a spectator or interpreter who is situated in a space-time frame of reference different from that of the events narrated. The *process* of narration culminates in the interpreter's immediate frame of reference, but it *refers* to events outside of that immediate situation. This is as true for my dinnertime recital of the little events of my day as it is for a performance of *King Lear* or *Swan Lake*, or a reading of *War and Peace*. Narration, then, rests upon the presence of a narrator or narrative medium (actors, book, film, etc.) and the absence of the events narrated. These events are present as fictions but absent as realities. Given this situation, it is possible to distinguish different kinds and qualities of narration by the varying extents to which they emphasize either that immediate process of narration (as an actor may draw attention to himself as performer or a writer to himself as stylist) or those mediated events themselves. Using our common critical terminology, it is possible to say that a narration is more fictional as it emphasizes the events narrated, more lyrical as it emphasizes its own language, and more rhetorical as it uses either language or events for some persuasive end.

Before looking more closely at the processes of narration, it may be useful to pause here and consider the relationship of narrative to theories of literature and literary value. The Russian formalists and the Prague school of structuralists, and in particular Roman Jakobson, have attempted to isolate the quality of "literariness" as a feature added to ordinary language. They have defined literariness as language calling attention to itself, or as a kind of message in which emphasis is placed on the form of the utterance rather than on its referential capacity. For the student of narrative, however, it is clear that this notion is applicable only to the lyrical dimension of an utterance. If narratives may be considered to be literary, they must be literary also in a way that is more purely narrative. Let me try to put this problem in a more concrete fashion.

We can begin by considering a question: What distinguishes a literary narrative from my recital of the events of my day? Is it a matter of the style of my performance—my language, voice, gesture, as opposed to those of a literary raconteur—or is it a matter of the events themselves—the trivial, loosely ordered events of my day as opposed to events of greater consequence shaped to a more esthetically satisfying pattern? The question (which need not be answered) reinforces the notion that there are two distinct formal dimensions to narrative utterances: a presentational form, which is immediate (language, gesture, etc.), and a represented form, which is at one remove from the level of performance itself. In a novel, for instance, there is the language of the author, at one level, and the representation of character, situation, and event at another. In a play there are the language of the author, the performance of the actor, and the deeds of the character to consider: three easily discerned levels at which form is perceptible. And film adds at least one level to these, just through the processes of photography itself: camera angle, lighting, focus, and so forth.

In a sense, each of these formal levels adds a certain amount of literariness to the process simply by existing. Take, for instance, a text that can be read as a book, enacted on a stage, or filmed and projected on a screen—like Shakespeare's *Henry V*. Each of the added levels of presentational style intensifies the literariness of the experience by its own artifice: language plus enactment plus photography. And the achieved fiction is *there* on the screen with a specificity that the printed text alone can never hope to match. The price for this intensity is a reduction in the interpretive richness of the written text—and this happens as every level is added. When the play is staged, each performance makes interpretive choices for the reader—but no two performances make all the same choices. When the story is filmed, all choices are final, which suggests that one ought to be very careful about confusing interpretive richness with the quality of literariness in any given work. Life itself, with all its quotidian contingency, provides the richest possible field for interpretation. Art reduces this field—drastically. And that is why we value it—not the only reason, but perhaps the main one. My example, of course, being a film based on an enactment of a particularly rich verbal text, is oversimple and may even be misleading in certain respects. Certainly I do not wish to suggest that verbal texts are rich and cinematic ones impoverished with respect to interpretability. Rather, it is my ultimate intention to indicate the different kinds of interpretation that verbal and cinematic texts entail, and to illustrate this with some brief examples drawn from contemporary American films. But first it will be necessary to return to some consideration of the general aspects of narrative behavior.

Any telling or recounting of a string of events may be called narration. But not every narration yields a narrative, and not every narrative makes a story. By becoming a story, or pretending to be a story, a narration arrives at literariness of the fictive kind. A story is a narration that attains a certain degree of completeness, and even a fragment of a story or an unfinished story will imply that completeness as an aspect of its informing principle—the intentionality that governs its construction. Given its linear, consecutive character, it is not surprising that film has come to be a predominantly narrative medium. That it should be dominated by stories, however, is somewhat more surprising, but dominated by stories it is, to a much greater extent than printed books are dominated by novels.

At this point it may be useful to review some terminology. A *narration* is a process of enactment or recounting that is a common feature of our cultural experience. We all do some of it every day. When this process is sufficiently coherent and developed to detach itself from the flux of cultural interchange, we perceive it as a *narrative*. As a perceived narrative begins to imply a special kind of pointedness or teleology, we recognize that it is a *story,* and we regard it with a certain set of expectations about its expressive patterning and its semantic content. We have a continuum here, like the color spectrum, which our perceptual mechanism breaks into discrete levels. And the level we recognize as "story" is distinguished by certain structural features in presentation which in turn require of the perceiver an active participation that I should like to call "narrativity." This word is at present used, by French critics primarily, to refer to a property of films themselves—their narrative quality. But the word seems a trifle misleading in English, in that it implies a more sentient character than we generally allow to an artifact. For this reason and some others, I should like to employ the word "narrativity" to refer to the process by which a perceiver actively constructs a story from the fictional data provided by any narrative medium. A fiction is presented to us in the form of a narration (a narrative text) that guides us as our own active narrativity seeks to complete the process that will achieve a story.

The nature of narrativity is to some extent culturebound. It is a matter of learned or acquired behavior, like the acquisition of a particular language, but it is based on a predisposition or potential of the human species to acquire this particular kind of behavior. In the contemporary Western world the culture of narrativity appears to be sufficiently homogeneous so that it may be considered in the way that a single language may be—as a systematic whole. We are only beginning to study "readers reading," as opposed to the texts that they read, so my remarks on narrativity will have to be rough and ready, based to a certain extent on intuitive extrapolations from my own experience as a reader and a teacher of reading. But it is also possible to base a study of narrativity at least partially upon texts, if we consider texts in various media. We need more than one medium because things that are left to the reader's narrativity in some media are presented directly in others. The arrival of film on the narrative scene has enabled us to perceive certain features of fiction more clearly because they are part of the narration in film, while they have only been part of the reader's narrativity in fiction. To take the most obvious instance, the visual quality of film reminds us forcibly of how much of fictional narrativity involves the supplying of physical details or the translating of verbal signs into images. Readers who are feeble at such visualizing often fail to realize important aspects of fictional texts. Film, of course, does not raise such problems of visualization. It raises other problems, which I shall consider later on. For the moment, it may be useful to break down a bit further the processes of esthetic interpretation.

The activities of readers and spectators in the face of artistic or recreational texts involve both a passive or automatic translation of semiotic conventions into intelligible elements and an active or interpretive rearrangement of textual signs into a significant structures. The automatic part of these operations is a matter of linguistic or semiotic competence and not of special interest to us upon this occasion; the interpretive part concerns us here. The interpreter of lyric poetry, for example, must of course know the language and the verbal conventions in which a poem is cast. But he must go beyond this level of competence to understand the poem. In particular, he must construct a situational structure from clues in the poem—who speaks, to whom, under what circumstances, and so forth—and he must also decompose the special linguistic features of the poetic lexicon, grammar, and syntax in order to comprehend them. He must measure poetic structures against the prosaic structures he needs to understand the deviant features of poetic utterance. He must supply missing parts of metaphors; he must acknowledge the ordinary words replaced by unusual ones in order to grasp the functions of the unusual ones; he must discover the fundamental syntactic structures in sentences that conceal aspects of those structures. In order to understand, he must explicate or unfold what is implicated or folded into the poem. And the poetic text must be designed to reward such interpretive activity. This activity is a matter of supplying semiotic features that the text requires for interpretation, of building a hermeneutic structure around the text itself. The poem is not the text alone but the text used to construct a complete and intelligible interpretation of it. A poem is a text that requires and rewards poetic procedures (or "poeticity") and its interpretation.

Similarly, a narrative is a text that requires and rewards narrativity. Narrativity involves a number of procedures of interpretive constructing, but one of these may be singled out as the most characteristic feature of this activity. Just as the lyric is characterized by the need to simplify its verbal constructions for interpretation, the narrative is characterized by a need to simplify certain elements in narration. We "make sense" of a poem by perceiving familiar sentence patterns within its unique verbal structure. We make sense of narration in a similar fashion, but at a different level of the text. In a story it is the order of events that concerns us more than the order of words. And our primary effort in attending to a narration is to construct a satisfying order of events. To do this we must locate or provide two features: temporality and causality.

Narrativity is based upon a mental operation similar to a logical fallacy: *post hoc ergo propter hoc*. What is a fallacy in logic is a principle of fiction: that a cause-and-effect relationship links the temporal elements in any narrative sequence. I am not suggesting that fiction itself is fallacious in some way, but rather that it is constructed so as to make this fallacy a feature of the fictional world. When we say that a work is episodic, for instance, we mean that the work frustrates the narrativitous urge for causal connection and we consider this a fictional deficiency (though obviously there may be other, nonfictional compensations in any given work). Above all, when we recognize a work as a story, we regard it as having a temporal sequentiality based on cause and effect. This means that if the events in a story are presented in their temporal sequence, much of our narrativity is devoted to establishing the causal connections between one event and the next. It means further that if the events themselves are presented out of temporal sequence, we seek first to arrive at an understanding of the true temporal sequence in order then to grasp the causal sequence informing the temporal. In the course of following even a simple fiction the processes of narrativity can be quite complex, as we separate the causal from the merely descriptive or contingent, as we seek to anticipate the future events in the causal patterns we discern, and we reconsider past events based on present understandings. The extraordinary popularity of detective fiction since Poe is based upon the way in which this fictional form incorporates the principles of narrativity within the narration itself. We follow the detective moving through time from crime to solution, while he, in turn, is in the process of constructing a narration of the crime itself from a set of clues encountered without their temporal and causal situations having been clarified. From discrete clues, he constructs a criminal narrative, which finally provides a verification or correction of our own narrativity. (See Tzvetan Todorov, *Poetics of Prose,* Chapter 3, for a full discussion of this.) Something like this pattern is as old as *Oedipus,* and is at least adumbrated in much drama and in melodramatic fiction. In the theater, the chronology of on-stage events tends toward brevity and direct temporal flow, but frequently generates revelations that belong to the time before the play began. There is often a story in a play which includes important events that precede the plot enacted on stage.

The strength of the human disposition toward simple narrativity can be measured in part through the mounting assaults upon that disposition in various modern and postmodern media. Pirandello and Brecht represent in theater two ways of trying to work against the spectator's impulse toward narrativity. Pirandello breaks illusion for esthetic reasons, to demonstrate the power of illusion, and finally to urge upon us the view that life itself is a matter of enactment and illusion. Brecht seeks to subvert narrativity to allow his theater ideological scope for the realization of ethical ends. And in film Resnais and Godard represent positions similar to Pirandello and Brecht in theater. We could find fictional analogues for these figures as well, in the labyrinths of Robbe-Grillet or the novelistic journalism of Hunter S. Thompson. Yet all these assaults on narrativity—and their ancestors in Cervantes, Calderón, Diderot, Sterne, and others—depend upon narrativity and could not function without it. It may even be that no long form of discourse can be received by a reader, spectator, or auditor unless it allows and encourages a certain amount of narrativity in its audience.

The nature of narrativity can be seen in another way. It is based not only upon what is a fallacy in logic but upon behavior that in psychology must be seen as neurotic or psychotic. Narrativity is a form of licensed and benign paranoia. (How many schoolchildren refer to the author of a book as "they" or "them"?) The interpreter of a narrative process assumes a purposefulness in the activities of narration which, if it existed in the world, would be truly destructive of individuality and personality as we know them. (I leave aside the question of whether this would be an improvement.) The spectator or reader of a narrative assumes that he is in the grip of a process controlled outside himself, designed to do things to him that he will be powerless to resist, and that all his struggles will only enmesh him further in the author's toils. Much of our impatience with inferior fiction comes from our loss of faith in the author's power. When he fails to anticipate our reactions and to lay traps for us into which we delightedly stumble, we begin to wonder if he is in control at all and to fear that we may have to move out of narrativity and into narration itself—or else simply return to entirely nonnarrative behavior.

A feature of narrativity is our desire to abandon certain dimensions of existence, certain quotidian responsibilities, and place ourselves under the illusionary guidance of a maker of narratives, upon whom we rely because we respect his powers. There is something very undemocratic about all this, and uncritical as well. Criticism begins when narrativity ceases. Life resumes when narrativity ceases. Call it escape or call it transcendence, narrativity is a pleasurable state of consciousness that is as different from other states as the dreaming part of sleep is from the other parts. This element of narrativity, which is perhaps its most fundamental and most primitive dimension, is a source of dissatisfaction to many contemporary writers and film makers. This quality of submission and abandon, which is so characteristic of narrativitous activity, has led some creators of narrative artifacts to try forcing the reader out of his familiar patterns of narrativity and into some more dynamic and tendentious attitude toward the text. The search for a "zero degree" of writing, in which the writer simply provides materials out of which a reader constructs a text, is, in the terms I have been using, an attempt to turn narrativity into narration itself. The ultimate form of this tendency would be a book with blank pages, or a silent concert (which John Cage has given us), an empty picture frame, a motion-picture screen lit by the lamp of the projector but showing only its own texture and perhaps the motes in the middle distance or the specks on the lens. These antiforms all have been or will be tried, but they are capable of little development. Even an encore to a silent concern presents a problem. And the zero degree of life is death.

I should like to suggest that the proper way for narrative artists to provide for their audiences an experience richer than submissive stupefaction is not to deny them the satisfactions of story but to generate for them stories that reward the most energetic and rigorous kinds of narrativity. It is possible, as Shakespeare knew, to provide some plain satisfactions for the simple or the weary, while also rewarding those who are ready to give a narrative the fullest attention of their mental and emotional powers. In the remaining portion of this chapter, I wish to turn my attention to the way film, in particular, can achieve this and is achieving this at present, even in works of what might be called the middle range, that do not aspire to the summits of esthetic approbation. In order to do this—and at the risk of covering overfamiliar ground for some of my readers—I shall begin with a brief review of the nature of cinematic signs.

As Christian Metz has made abundantly clear, film and narrative have such a powerful affinity that their relationship assumes a supreme naturalness. When, in the eighteenth century, Lessing sought so elaborately to contrast the mimetic possibilities of verbal narration and pictorial representation, he neatly (doubtless too neatly) divided the world between them—assigning to the sequential, arbitrary signs of fiction the narration of actions, and to the simultaneous, motivated signs of painting the description of objects and persons. If he were brought back to life today he would recognize in cinema the reconciliation of the parts of his divided world, for the motion-picture film gives us objects and persons moving and enacting in a visual system of narration that combines the powers of poetry and painting in an extraordinary synthesis.

The product of this synthesis, however, is a very different thing from verbal narration, more so than we sometimes realize, and in a way that Lessing would understand—different because the signs in cinema function differently from the signs of verbal fiction. In the language of verbal narration each sign is first interpreted as a concept or category, and then, where this is relevant and possible, connected to a referent of some sort. Thus, if I say to you "There's a dog on the lawn," you translate the sound-image "dog" into some canine category of your own, and if you are moved to look out the window and see for yourself, you may finally perceive a specific referent that will supplant the conceptual category in your interpretive operation. If I provide you with a fictional dog, however, your concretization of the empty category will depend on an interaction between my narration and your narrativity. If I say, "He's lifting his leg," your image must lift a leg; preferably a hind one, but the choice of leg is left up to you, unless and until I provide you with new verbal data that force you to correct your image.

If, on the other hand—or leg—I present you with a cinematic dog, the signifying process is entirely different. You are confronted with a sign tightly tied to a specific referent, which you then may relate to a categorical concept or a set of such concepts by a process that may be partly conscious and partly not. I may misdirect you, if I can use words in my film, calling a male dog Lassie, and if the dog is sufficiently woolly or the camera work and editing sufficiently adroit, you may never detect the imposture, and thus assign the referent to a category that is fictionally correct but factually false—a problem that can hardly come up in verbal narration, where if I call a dog Lassie you are obliged to provide her with all the proper equipment or to leave parts of her blank until I direct your attention to them.

The point of this excursion into sign language is to suggest that though the "same narrative" may be presented in both verbal and cinematic form, the narration and the narrativity will be extremely different. This is why my earlier example of *Henry V* was to a certain extent misleading. Since the verbal part of a play is entirely oral, it may be completely reproduced in a film. In a novel, however, much of the language is busy with description and reflection, which must be eliminated in cinematic translation. Even voice-over narration in films made from novels, which is used very effectively in a good film like *Farewell My Lovely* or a great one like *Jules et Jim*, is highly selective when compared to the total verbiage of the book. These differences in narration correspond to important differences in narrativity. The reader's narrative processes in dealing with printed fiction are mainly oriented toward visualization. This is what the reader must supply for a printed text. But in cinematic narrative the spectator must supply a more categorial and abstract narrativity. This is one reason film criticism is frequently more interesting than literary criticism. A well-made film requires interpretation, while a well-made novel may only need understanding. There is a redundancy in providing a verbal gloss for a verbal object that does not apply when the object is significantly visual.

Some movements in contemporary fiction can be seen as attempts to acquire a cinematic opacity and freedom from conceptual thinking. Alain Robbe-Grillet has tried very hard to be a camera and has produced some interesting verbal *tours de force*. But these experiments in writing against the grain of verbal narration are limited in their developmental possibilities. A writer who wants to be a camera should probably make a movie (as Robbe-Grillet has, of course, with mixed results). Makers of narrative films can also work against the grain, and films have been made which try to conceptualize so much that they founder in seas of rhetoric. These two different narrative media require and must encourage two different kinds of narrativity—though both admit of great intensity and great complexity. Before concluding, I should like to explore some aspects of narrativity in a few American films, as an illustration of the processes I have been discussing, perhaps too abstractly. These processes involve the conceptualization of images and the construction of frameworks of causality and value around such concepts.

A few years ago I found myself moved in very different ways to different kinds of narrativity by the images of America presented in three films: *The Great Waldo Pepper, Godfather II,* and *The Parallax View.* Having seen each film only once, I am in no position to argue their merits vigorously or to analyze them with any pretensions to depth and rigor. But each of them proved striking to me, and left me with residues of narrativity that have become a part of my cognitive apparatus.

Waldo Pepper is a charming film, perhaps too conscious of its charm. It summons up an America already coded for us by Norman Rockwell—but it transcends this quality on several occasions. In the crowd scenes around the fatal plane crash we find Rockwell's world metamorphosed into something like Nathanael West's— with an economy and power far beyond the ponderous Westian fidelities of the cinematic *Day of the Locust.* Suddenly the blood lust, the brutality behind the placid surface of mid-America bursts through the Rockwellian facade, and it is all the more convincing because of the sincerity with which that facade had been established in the film. In the processes of my own narrativity, continuing long after the viewing itself was completed, still continuing, joining the images of the great metafilm I am constructing in my mind, other images have come to dominate my recollection of that film. Not the Rockwellian faces, not even the marvelous aerial acrobatics, but features of landscape and humanity that are closer to Grant Wood than to Rockwell. In particular, I see a frame house, a tree, a person or two at home in these surroundings, and beyond them the fields and the sky. The camera is stationary or moving slowly, and the sense of peace, of man's harmony with nature, is overwhelming. These images generate in me the same feeling I experience when I go back to Iowa, where you can smell the fertility of the land and understand how people can love it, and how that farmer's love for the earth must transcend national boundaries and go back for centuries to beyond the beginning of history. That this sense of land should be so strong in a film about the sky, about restlessness, about people who find no resting place on the ground, is important. It is a measure of a kind of complexity in a film that is in many respects simple, and it is a complexity that comes from a loving attention to images which invite us to go through them to the meanings behind them.

Our narrativity with respect to a film like *Waldo Pepper* begins with a simple attempt to register the images, to categorize them and assign them value according to whatever cultural codes we have available. Where I use Norman Rockwell and Grant Wood, someone else might operate with different paradigms, which might not carry any labels at all. But in any case, as we proceed along the narrative track of the film, we construct the story of Waldo himself from the incidents presented to us, and we charge that story with value and emotion in very complex ways. What I wish to suggest here is that a part of that vital and complex process by which we accomplish this energizing of the narration depends upon such things as our codifying and assigning value to particular images. In this case, Waldo's fate is as it is because his life is torn between the placidity of that prairie landscape, tamed by man, and the pettiness and cruelty of man as a social being. Waldo cannot accept the placidity of the one side of his culture and he despises the mundane cupidity and sensationalism of the other. His lies and his flights are both attempts to transcend these realities, to construct a mythic world that he can comfortably inhabit. But one way or another, planes must come down. Myths may be created but they cannot be lived.

Some devotees of film may object to my discussion as moving too far from the reality of dissolves and jump cuts to some airy realm of thematic speculation. But this is precisely what we must do in the realization of a narrative film. The cinematic world invites—even requires—conceptualization. The images presented to us, their arrangements and juxtapositioning, are narrational blueprints for a fiction that must be constructed by the viewer's narrativity.

The images of America in *Godfather II* are different from those of *Waldo Pepper*, of course, as different as Little Italy from Nebraska or Las Vegas from Keokuk. But the images evoke similar processes of narrativity in our minds. For me the scenes of Ellis Island are worth a stack of history books. One long shot in particular, the camera tracking slowly past the immigrant hordes, labeled and herded like cattle, brought the dream and the reality of America into vertiginous proximity. Some of my ancestors stood in those lines, and I felt closer to them as I watched than I had ever felt before. The slow camera, the warm lighting, the hopeful patience of the crowds provided an image closer to the heart of this country than any *Mayflower* or Plymouth Rock. The film, of course, is about the betrayal of this dream: the mafioso in his fortress, the senator in his whorehouse, the conference of thugs and politicians in Batista's Cuba. These images must be set next to those patient lines of immigrants for the film's full irony to be achieved. But once we grasp them they remain with us for a long time.

The Parallax View is less highly regarded than the other two and was, I believe, less successful commercially. But for me it is a film of extraordinary interest despite its weaknesses—and to a certain extent because of them. It attempted two remarkable narrative feats. It took the paranoia that lies benevolently at the heart of the narrative process itself and the other paranoia that threatens to overwhelm our national life and tried to make them congruent, and it undertook a single scene requiring the most intense narrativity I can recall encountering in a film. The picture provides a story that postulates a conspiracy behind the assassinations of various liberal political figures and satirizes the complacency or complicity of the inquiries into those assassinations. All the characters in the film who begin to perceive this plot against America die violently, and the last heroic defender is trapped into a situation where he is himself taken to be an assassin and is finally killed by those truly guilty, who are pretending to aid in his arrest. It is a chilling film, pointedly and scandalously close to actual contemporary events. It shares a view of America with the frighteningly irrational readers of scandal magazines and the uncritical devotees of paranoid conspiracy theories. As a film, its lack of popular success stems from the fact that its audience could not accept the slaughter of their protagonist. In the formulas of popular fiction, this film called for a victorious hero who saved the country from a wicked gang of conspirators. By accepting the paranoia latent in a part of the mass audience while rejecting the power fantasy and wish fulfillment that regularly accompany it, the film alienated its most likely audience. And of course those who consider themselves above such things were disqualified from the beginning.

The film had other problems—in pacing and in the logic of its storytelling, leaning too heavily on the invisible masters of conspiracy to tie together the loose ends of its plot, encouraging a sloppy and careless narrativity in the viewer. But it did give us one extraordinary scene, in which the intrepid protagonist, who is trying to infiltrate the conspiracy, faces a futuristic personality test. To qualify as an apprentice assassin he must demonstrate that he has the emotional profile of an extremely psychotic individual. The test consists of his being strapped into an electronic chair which monitors his reactions while he is shown slides calculated to produce strong emotional effects upon him: authority figures, sex objects, flags, scenes of violence and brutality, mom-type ladies, homosexuals, apple pie, Captain America—all in a rapid sequence of repetitions and juxtapositions. Our protagonist, to pass the test, must try to generate the appropriate involuntary reactions for a paranoid psychopath, and we, in our own chairs watching the same slides, are inevitably drawn to assist him empathetically by trying to force the appropriate reactions out of our own nervous systems. The result is a kind of mind-blowing sensory overload, a short-circuiting of a narrativity asked to accomplish too much too fast. The vagueness of the monitoring itself, the absence of rules for this game, indicates that the makers of the film were not in imaginative control of their own conception. Thus, the film repeatedly attempts to allow a real and malevolent paranoia to substitute for the benign paranoia at the heart of narrative activity. The film tries to hide its own imaginative inadequacies behind one of its inadequately conceived fictions. This is truly an instructive failure, for we see ideas that might have functioned powerfully reduced to the level of sensational gimmicks before our eyes.

In these three glances into the processes of cinematic narrativity I have been trying to suggest the power and importance of conceptualization by the viewer in the realization of narrative films. There is, of course, much more to cinematic narrative than this. And there is much less, too. Some aspects of narrative film are simply matters of stimulus and response, in which conceptualization is held to a minimum. This, I take it, is a useful definition of pornography, whether it is the pornography of pleasure or of pain. We need no very elaborate concepts of erotic or brutal acts to be "moved" by enactments of them—and even more "moved" by photographs of the actuality. But such motion, however violent, is not derived from any narrative process. Presumably to see someone tortured or gratified sexually before our eyes would be even more "moving," and to play the principal role in such a situation ourselves would be the most "moving" condition of all. And this would not be a narrative experience anymore. It would be life, not fiction.

Film, because it excels all other narrative media in its rendition of material objects and the actions of creatures, is the closest to actuality, to undifferentiated thoughtless experience. Literature, beginning in language, must exert extraordinary pains to achieve some impression of the real. For this reason written fiction has almost always used some notion of realism or verisimilitude as an evaluative standard. For film, the problem is different. It must achieve some level of reflection, of conceptualization, in order to reach its optimum condition as narrative. The best narrative films have always accomplished this, and they have done so cinematically, through scenes and images that induce an appropriate narrativity in their audiences.

5

A SEMIOTIC APPROACH TO IRONY IN DRAMA AND FICTION

"In the country of the blind, the one-eyed man is king."
                                                    Old Saying

I would like to begin with a brief excerpt from a literary text, a short story by H. G. Wells called "The Country of the Blind." In the story a sighted person wanders into a remote village where all the inhabitants have been blind for generations. Keeping the old adage in mind, the sighted man expects to become master among the blind, but events do not work out that way, and he becomes a prisoner, thought by his captors to be mad. At one point he challenges one of his captors:

> "My time will come," he said.
> "You'll learn," the blind man answered. "There is much to learn in the world."
> "Has no one told you, 'In the Country of the Blind the One-eyed Man is King'? "
> "What is blind?" asked the blind man carelessly over his shoulder.

This passage, like the whole story, gives me much pleasure. There are many reasons for this. I like the way the tale is structured as a thought experiment growing out of the matrix provided by the old adage and Plato's exemplum of The Cave. I like the way Wells extrapolates from the matrix with his deft combination of logic and imagination. I like all these things, but it seems to me impossible to account finally for my pleasure in this text without recourse to the concept of irony. The macro-structure of the story is a negation of the old saw about the country of the blind that is the story's matrix. This is narrative or dramatic irony. The sighted protagonist bases his expectations on the adage, and the events betray these expectations. It is a negation, moreover, that generates a new meaning. It effectively rewrites the adage: "In the country of the blind, the one-eyed man is considered mad."

This is not simply saying No to the old proverb. It involves a creative activity or recoding beyond the initial negation. Does the notion of irony as a figure of narrative discourse apply only to the negation of the adage, or to the rewriting of it as well? Let me reduce this macro-structure to the level of a proposition. Take the original adage and a simple rewriting of it by means of a single substitution:

In the country of the blind the one-eyed man is king.
In the country of the blind the one-eyed man is crazy.

Do we have a trope here? If so, what trope is it? The process at work in the story as a whole covers more than this propositional version does, of course, and we must be aware of that. We should also be aware that the original adage is itself a trope. It is allegorical. It is not really about countries of the blind, which do not exist, but about the relative superiority of a little over none at all—in all aspects of life. It could be rewritten about the country of the deaf or the country of the breadless or the country of the legless and so on and on and still carry much the same meaning at the allegorical level of abstraction.

What Wells's story does, then, is to take the allegorical quality of the proverb and literalize it remorselessly. It turns the figurative "country of the blind" into a mimetic or, more precisely, diegetic one. At this level, irony is an antitrope. As such, we must still class it among those creative or playful uses of language that give pleasure to all those who must regularly use language in a less figurative way.

But there is another level of the text we must examine before leaving it. One line in the quoted passage gives me a particular pleasure: "'What is blind?' asked the blind man." My pleasure in the line comes partly from the way it compresses so neatly the larger issues of the story, but there is also a distinctly pleasing quality in my experience that I want to attribute to another sort of complexity in the line. The word "blind" is used in two ways. To the blind man it is not even a word but simply a strange combination of phonemes, the babbling of a madman. To the sighted man in the story, to the narrator, the author, the reader, the critic, the critic's readers, and so forth—to all who know English, including those who read it in Braille—"blind" is a word with a meaning. But this is not simply a case of one person asking another to define his terms. The blind man's question is not purely metalingual—neither for him nor for his sighted auditor—and especially, not for us. The blind man's ignorance of the disability that is his very defining characteristic for the others, underlined by the text's bland repetition of the word he asks about in its own discourse, is most assuredly ironic. At any rate, we have no other word for this verbal phenomenon. This is an irony of situation or viewpoint. It stems from the double use of the word "blind," but it is not *in* the word, it is in the disparity between the two codes, which makes the same signal noise in one and a sign in the other. This is the synchronic mode of narrative irony, as the disappointment of the protagonist's expectations is the diachronic mode. These can both be brought down to the level of words in the text, but the irony is not in the words. It is in the diegesis (diachronic) and in the discourse (synchronic).

I have been stressing pleasure in this discussion because pleasure offers us another approach to the whole question of what literature is. To say that a text is literary to the extent that it offers the reader pleasure is to make a simple but powerful statement, to claim a position that could be held for a long time against the severe attacks that it would be sure to inspire. Personally, I would not hesitate to say it—I do say it, in fact—but it seems to me more important to go beyond that position and take the risks of trying to say *how* literary pleasure works.

The sources of pleasure in literary discourse can be defined as matters of communicative capacity. Literary texts offer readers a chance to use a fuller range of their interpretive abilities than do nonliterary texts. The reader's narrativity, as it generates and orders a diegesis from the textual blueprint of a novel, is one example of this. The reader's poeticity, as we may call it, working upon the figurative language of a text, is another. The neo-Freudians, especially Jacques Lacan and his circle, have reminded us that Jakobson's major poetic figures, metaphor and metonymy, are very close in meaning to Freud's condensation and displacement—as Jakobson himself observed. The unconscious speaks in these figures to avoid the censorship of consciousness, and in such discourse the repressed finds its expression, bringing the speaker pleasure. Thus—vastly abbreviated—runs the theory. But the theory does not quite account for the pleasure we take in figures as such, a pleasure that has as much to do with the conscious production of meaning as with unconscious expression.

Irony is a way of avoiding censorship, too, whether the censor is a politician or the superego. It is, in fact, much like the Freudian "negation" (*Verneinung*), which is the device that allows us to say "I don't want to upset you" when we intend, consciously or not, to do just that. It has never been easy to incorporate irony into the field of figures or tropes, for reasons that semiotic studies may help us understand. While metaphor and metonymy are expressed and understood primarily at the semantic level of discourse, irony depends to an extraordinary degree on the pragmatics of situation. In speech, irony will often be signaled by the nonverbal parts of utterance (intonation or gesture), while metaphor and metonymy are virtually independent of these features. Metaphor is rooted in the naming function of language, while irony is based on the communicative function. They use rather different features of communicative skill, and appeal to rather different temperaments, which is perhaps why many excellent writers tend to produce texts dominated by one or the other, rather than deploying both equally. Because it is rooted in the nonverbal part of communication, irony is preeminently the figure of narrative and dramatic texts, as metaphor is of lyric texts. In fact, for many ironists, the contrast between what is said and what is done is the basis of ironic structure, since words are allied with appearance and deeds with reality.

In reinstating irony at the center of a discussion of literary texts, I do not mean to invest it with a formalist or New Critical closure of these texts that would turn them into works. I shall not be talking about self-contradictions or ambiguities that paralyze meaning and allow the reader or spectator a purely aesthetic contemplation of a text. Far from it. For irony, of all figures, is the one that must always take us out of the text and into codes, contexts, and situations. It is in fact precisely this tendentiousness of irony that makes it an interesting semiotic problem—to illustrate which I have chosen several texts drawn from different genres, periods, and cultures in the past two centuries of Western literature.

In May of 1777, while the English were attempting to suppress a trifling rebellion of their North American colonies, a more amusing event took place in London, where a new play opened. The play was a great success and it has continued to have successes right up to the present day, despite the fact that, as a recent critic has complained, it is "simply a very brilliant stage piece," "conventional," and without a "real point of view." The idea of a highly successful play about nothing sounds almost Mallarméan, but we are talking here, of course, about Richard Sheridan's *School for Scandal*, a comedy of manners in a recognizably English tradition that extends from Wycherley to Wilde.

The most admired scene in this much admired play is act 4, scene 3, known as the screen scene. Let me refresh your memory about it just a bit. In the play there is a fortune to be bestowed by a rich uncle on one of his two nephews, Charles and Joseph Surface. Charles is a bit wild, drinking and gambling too much, but honest and good-hearted. Joseph, on the other hand, is a man of sentiment—which is to say that he has a fine-sounding and pious phrase for every occasion but is in fact mean-spirited and unscrupulous. The play thus poses a problem in ironic terms. There are surfaces to be seen through here, and the rich uncle returning from the Indies must determine, with the aid of his old friend Sir Peter Teazle, which nephew should be his beneficiary. This is complicated by the fact that Sir Peter Teazle, an old husband with a young bride, is misled by the surfaces of the two nephews and does not realize that sentimental Joseph is actually trying to seduce Lady Teazle.

The screen scene begins in the house of the sentimental Joseph Surface, who is ordering a servant to place a screen in front of his library window, because his "opposite neighbor is a maiden lady of so curious a temper." The screen is thus to be used to obstruct vision, to prevent an act of spectation. But we, the spectators to the play, are positioned on the other side of the room, and no screen will be placed to obstruct *our* vision. Joseph's reason for placing the screen is in one sense merely Sheridan's excuse for getting it on stage, but it also heightens the spectators' sense of privilege, of voyeuristic pleasure. We are about to witness a seduction, and our knowledge of Joseph's intentions provides us with a key that should interpret ironies to come.

Enter Lady Teazle. Sir Peter's wife arrives and Joseph begins trying to reason her into adultery, arguing first that since there is already some scandal whispered about her (which he knows well since he has been having it whispered and directed at his brother), and since the scandal has made her husband suspicious of her, that she "owes it to the honor of her sex" to actually deceive him. To this he adds the wonderful argument that her husband should never be deceived about her, so that if he suspects her of adultery she should "be frail in compliment to *his* discernment." In other words, she should make the facts conform to his mistaken reading of the surface of reality for the sake of *his* honor.

Sheridan is building his play upon the theme of irony itself, the differences between appearances and realities, words and deeds. Just as Joseph begins to move from words to deeds, though the lady is still debating her response, his servant enters to announce her husband, Sir Peter, who is on his way up to the room in which the seduction is occurring. With a cry of "What will become of me now, Mr. Logic?" Lady Teazle hides behind the screen as her husband enters.

At this point things become especially interesting for the spectators. We watch the two men on stage, knowing that one speaks innocently, unaware that his wife is overhearing him, and the other duplicitously. And we interpret not only for ourselves but for the other spectator behind the screen. Thus the ironies multiply and with them our spectatorial pleasure. The conversation, which is delicious in its ironies, cannot be recounted here, but its subject matter is partly Sir Peter's suspicion that his wife may be having an affair with the absent brother, Charles. Before long the servant enters again to say that Charles himself has arrived and insists on coming up. Sir Peter then gets the brilliant idea of hiding, so that Joseph can test Charles in conversation about his supposed interest in Sir Peter's wife. At this point Sir Peter goes to hide behind the screen—raising the comic expectations of the audience—but Joseph stops him just in time. Sir Peter insists he has seen a skirt behind the screen and Joseph says that a French milliner who was visiting him has hidden herself behind it, whereupon Sir Peter enters a handy closet.

Enter Charles to play a scene with Joseph before an enlarged audience of voyeurs: Lady Teazle, who knows that her husband is also listening, Sir Peter, who does not know of Lady Teazle's presence, and of course, all of us. Joseph, now playing to more audiences than he can conveniently deceive, is in a difficult situation. And we, interpreting every word as Lady Teazle must and as Sir Peter must, are in a supremely privileged and pleasurable situation as we correlate the multiple ironies being generated before us. In his honesty Charles accuses Joseph of paying court to Lady Teazle, at which point Joseph is forced to begin dissolving the layers of irony by telling Charles that Sir Peter is in the closet. Charles shames Sir Peter into coming out and Sir Peter admits his error. At this point Joseph's crony Lady Sneerwell arrives and he goes downstairs to prevent her from coming up and complicating the situation further. Sir Peter then tells Charles about the supposed milliner in hiding and Charles tips over the screen, revealing Lady Teazle, just as Joseph returns. They all stand mute for a moment as Charles asks them questions, throwing back at Sir Peter and Joseph some phrases of their own that take on a new meaning in this ironic context, after which Charles leaves.

At this point the stage directions say: "They stand for some time looking at each other." This, I submit, is one of the great moments of pure stagecraft in the history of theatre. And it is wordless. The looks they exchange offer wonderful scope to the actress and actors involved. And the audience is offered wonderful scope for interpretive activity. All the layers of ironic perception are now allowed to discharge into laughter and applause. Accounts of the first performances in Drury Lane Theatre say that the noise in the playhouse was unparalleled, startling people in the streets outside.

Having achieved this, Sheridan had left himself the problem of finding a speech good enough to start the play going again. He proved completely equal to the task. The silence is broken by Joseph, who says: "Sir Peter—notwithstanding I confess that appearances are against me—if you will afford me your patience—I make no doubt but I shall explain everything to your satisfaction."

Ever the man of words, Joseph is still confident that they will prove adequate to subdue mere "appearances." But all theatrical works, and this play in particular, are built upon an ironic structure of spectation in which disparities of word and deed are quickly observed, so that what is enacted is privileged over what is recounted, "appearance" over "explanation." The spectators are not passive observers of a tableau or dumb show but active interpreters of a dynamic process. The written text is simply a blueprint for the actors, and the actors depend on the interpretive ability of the audience. The moment of silent exchange of looks near the end of the screen scene is a great theatrical moment because it can be sustained as long as the actors can mime and the audience interpret additional nuances of meaning. If the audience is dull, the actors must get the scene moving again quickly; if the audience is alert, and the actors are skilled, that meaningful silence on stage can be prolonged for an astonishingly long time.

What is operative in such a scene is not only irony, of course, but the fundamental irony of spectation is at the bottom of it all— the fact that different viewpoints produce different feelings and that surfaces never tell the whole story. In watching theater we are always finally aware that it is all a game, a play, that beneath the surface of costume, makeup, voice, and manner there lives another being who is not the person whose life we are following. Theater depends on separating the actor from the actant. Without this we are participating in a ceremony, not observing a drama. The irony of double vision is what makes the drama possible, and this, in turn, depends upon the development of interpretive skill in dramatic audiences.

Sheridan's play, however, also depends upon a code of values so simple that almost any audience could be induced to share it. Deceit is bad, adultery is bad; honesty and generosity are good. There is nothing problematic here, for the very good reason that anything of that sort would interfere with the laughter the play is designed to produce. The irony is directed at a perfect comic villain, Joseph Surface, and it is based upon the deepest and simplest aspects of a social code that in the England of 1777 had hardly begun to be questioned. The play works today because it offers us a world so easily entered, however quaint we may feel it to be, like the fairy-tale world of a marionette show.

In Balzac's short novel of 1833, *Eugénie Grandet*, we enter a very different world, in which irony works in a very different way. We are moving from the stage to the book, of course, as well as from England to France, and from the eighteenth century to the nineteenth. It is an enormous change from the comedy of manners to the kind of narration that we have learned to call both "realistic" and "omniscient" without being as troubled as we should by any conflict between those two terms. I choose this kind of text and this kind of irony because I feel that they represent a certain extreme development in narrative—one kind of irony being stretched about as far as it will go. This stretching is apparent everywhere in the text but perhaps nowhere more so than in the "postface" to the first edition, which has been unaccountably omitted from the "complete and unabridged" American version by Lowell Blair (Bantam Classic). Here Balzac claims for himself the status of humble copyist from life. In his ringing phrase: "Ici, nulle invention." But only two paragraphs later he concludes the postface and the book with the following words:

> Parmi les femmes, Eugénie Grandet sera peut-être un type, celui des dévouements jetés à travers les orages du monde et qui s'y engloutissent comme une noble statue enlevée à la Grèce et qui, pendant le transport, tombe à la mer où elle demeurera toujours ignorée.

The floridity of this language cannot help acting as a gloss on the earlier phrase. No invention? Perhaps not, in this epic simile, but certainly a good deal of embellishment.

Balzac invokes the image of himself as a painter from life, a humble miniaturist, and finally of a Praxiteles of the provinces, but all of these images of the writer as plastic artist serve only to beg the main question, which is how words can in any sense "copy" an existence that extends so far beyond the verbal. In fact, what words most clearly cannot do is "copy" nonverbal things. In order to present the life of Saumur accurately, Balzac surrounds his tiny story with heaps of discourse. Only in this way does he feel confident that he can depict adequately his provincial scene. In his preface of 1833 (also omitted from the American text) he is at pains to justify the author's right to be generous with the "longueurs" required by the "circle of minutiae in which he is obliged to move."

We may seem to be far from irony here, but we are not. Balzacian irony in a work like *Eugénie Grandet* is precisely a function of the author's freedom of movement in relation to the characters' limitations. The most revealing phrase in the book comes casually, after Balzac has been describing the ready acquiescence of the three women in Grandet's household to his miserly bullying. After telling us that Grandet believed himself very generous toward his wife, the Balzacian narrator adds: "Les philosophes qui rencontrent des Nanon, des madame Grandet, des Eugénie ne sont-ils pas en droit de trouver que l'ironie est le fond du caractère de la Providence?" Well. Irony may or may not be the most basic characteristic of Providence, but it is certainly the basis for omniscient narration. And the road from Eugénie Grandet to Emma Bovary and Hardy's Tess lies open before us in this aside of Balzac's.

The ironic power of the Balzacian narrator is felt at every level from the fable itself to the discourse that falls upon the characters like the snuff that speckles the shirts of the three Cruchots. But nowhere is it more apparent than when the narrator moves from character to character, from body to mind, to exhibit the cross-purposes, the deceptions, and the petty selfishnesses that surround Eugénie. Especially in the first large scene, where the Cruchot and Des Grassin clans are assembled for Eugénie's birthday, each hoping to promote the cause of their candidate for the hand of the heiress, when Charles Grandet arrives from Paris.

One could linger over this for some time, noticing the ironic shifts of viewpoint, but in the interest of brevity I wish to consider just a sentence and a half. Adolphe Des Grassins has just greeted Eugénie and is presenting his birthday gift:

> ...et lui offrit une boîte à ouvrage dont les ustensiles étaient en vermeil, véritable marchandise de pacotille, malgré l'écusson sur lequel un E. G. gothique assez bien gravé pouvait faire croire à une façon très-soignée. En l'ouvrant, Eugénie eut une de ces joies inespérés et complètes qui font rougir, tresailler, trembler d'aìse les jeunes filles.

The irony is essentially that Eugénie is so moved by such a trifle, something silver plated, in the narrator's discourse "marchandise de pacotille," stuff from a pedlar's pack—or the equivalent. From the disparity in the evaluation of this object by Eugénie and by the narrator, enriched in a moment by the reaction of the Cruchots, the irony emerges, somewhat as it might in a play. But in no play could the irony *depend* upon the authority of such a narrator's evaluation; whereas in Balzac's novel much of the discourse is devoted precisely to establishing that authority: for example, the "rather well engraved" ("assez bien gravé") initials that could fool someone less knowledgeable than our narrator, and the formulaic "un de ces... qui," which are as necessary to Balzacian discourse as epithets are to Homer. The phrase "one of those... joys which" points not to the blushing and trembling of the character but to the encyclopedic and truly providential omniscience of the narrator—upon whose character the irony of the text is founded.

It is partly because he is not as sure of his audience as was Sheridan, but also because he is trying to do so much more that Balzac must generate such a bullying, self-assured, and superior narrative discourse. The irony *must* illuminate Eugénie for us. That a genuine emotion should be induced in her by a piece of meretricious trash presented by a young fool with the most cynical aims in mind—and not just a genuine emotion but an overpowering one, causing her to "rougir, tresailler, trembler"—must not result in our *smiling at* Eugénie with ironic superiority. To prevent this the narrator is ever at our ear, turning the irony into sentiment or redirecting it toward those around her. It is not just Balzac whose narrative discourse functions in this way. We can recognize a similar technique in Dickens as well, and in Flaubert at times (however refined and polished), and through the whole realistic-naturalistic tradition. The discourse of Balzac needs its omniscience not only to generate its irony but also to prevent the reader from interpreting that irony with too great a freedom. This is why Sheridan's piece of theatrical fluff is still as fresh as a daisy, while Balzac's earnest pieties meet greater resistance with each passing year. We do, as Nathalie Sarraute told us, live in an age of suspicion, and we can hardly help resisting a narrator who continually does our thinking for us and pretends to an omniscience we find it less and less easy to credit.

Most of us resist privately by reading Balzac less, or more openly by subjecting him to the deconstructive attentions of the Nouvelle Critique. One of the more striking pieces of resistance to Balzac appeared in *The New Yorker* on 17 August 1968. It was called "Eugénie Grandet," and took the form of a brief reworking of Balzac's story in a text, with illustrations, of just two pages, constructed by Donald Barthelme. The text begins with a summary of the plot, attributed to a *"Thesaurus of Book Digests,"* and continues with fragments of an actual English translation, with absurd summaries, parodies, and illustrations, to the point where it becomes difficult to distinguish the portions of the "original" from the newly constructed absurdities. Barthelme forces us to reconsider aspects of Balzac's text in this new light. So now we have two "texts" of *Eugénie Grandet* and precisely where Balzac tried to narrow the focus of irony with his insistent omı ̖cient discourse, Barthelme makes a new opening for irony. We must see Eugénie herself, the book, and Balzac, in more than one way, through more than one discourse. The very insistence of Balzac's discourse has not only enabled but begotten the ironic response of Barthelme.

Consider briefly some of Barthelme's devices. He inserts, out of chronological order, a description of old Grandet's death:

> Old Grandet clutches his chest, and capitulates. Eight hundred thousand a year! He gasps. A death by gasping.

This is pure invention, of course, linking Grandet's death to the income achieved by his daughter years after, when she is a virginal widow. It is also pure verbal play. He *"capit*ulates" because he is a *capit*alist. Sound is affecting—and debasing—sense. Earlier Barthelme has given us another fragment:

> "Here's a million and a half francs, Judge," Eugénie said, drawing from her bosom a certificate for a hundred shares in the Bank of France.

This absurd event, combining like the other a huge sum of money and the human breast in a ridiculous way, happens to be an exact quotation from the English translation, which is itself quite accurate here. But placing the absurd invented discourse and the genuine discourse on the same plane generates new ironies for the alert reader.

Barthelme's text has in fact no discourse of its own. It is a collage of discourses presented without reference to an interpretive center. One of the longest and most puzzling fragments in the entire piece is apparently an interview between a member of the Grandet family and a man who has come to paint Eugénie's portrait. In the course of the interview the painter says he is an American whose name is John Graham and whose dates are 1881 to 1961. Leaving aside the absurdity of a man knowing his own dates, Graham's are in no way contiguous with Eugénie's, since Balzac ends her story in the present time of his own narration: 1833. The interview ends after Graham has showed samples of his portraits of people in the wild West:

> "Why are they all cross-eyed?"
> "Well, that's just the way I do it. I don't see anything wrong with that. It often occurs in nature."
> "But *every one* is...."
> "Well, what's so peculiar about that? I just like... that's just the way I do it. I *like*...."

End of interview. But how are we to interpret it? Balzac was fond of comparing himself to a painter, a copyist from life. What has that to do with this specialist in the cross-eyed portrait? Are we *supposed* to bring this passage into an absurd juxtaposition with Balzac? Are we *supposed* to conclude that Balzac had his own little preferences which took him as far from being an accurate copyist as a painter who crosses the eyes of all his subjects? Is this a profound utterance about *style* in art?

We are not *supposed* to reach any particular conclusion. We are allowed to perform interpretive games with these materials, but we will have to take a large share of responsibility for the results. We are afloat in irony here and must learn to swim in it or drown. It is reasonable to see this as a protest against the weight of literary history, against the very existence of Balzac, against the idea of omniscience and the coercion or manipulation of the reader that inevitably accompanies it. In our time, writers have turned the irony of written discourse against discourse itself, to a greater extent than ever before, as the names of Kafka, Beckett, Borges, and Nabokov will remind us, without adding the host of younger writers like Barthelme himself who have followed this path.

Looking back over the three ironic writers we have been considering, we can draw a simple conclusion. In the classic comedy of Sheridan we had an irony that needed no authoritative discourse to focus it but drew upon simple principles of value and a clear social consensus; in Balzac we found an irony that was controllable only at the price of introducing a highly coercive and manipulative discourse; and in Barthelme and other contemporary writers we have discourse that invites its own ironies upon itself, through the deliberate introduction into both story and discourse of gaps, contradictions, and absurdities. There need be no question of a progression here. All we can say is that for better or worse, this is our age, and any attempt to create a discourse free from irony within its epistemological confines will not be easy. In the country of the Ironic, Omniscience itself appears absurd.

6

SEMIOTIC APPROACHES TO JOYCE'S "EVELINE"

The purpose of this chapter is a simple one. I wish to argue, and to demonstrate as well as possible, that certain semiotic approaches to fictional texts, each incomplete in itself, can be combined in a manner that facilitates the practical criticism of fiction. The three approaches I wish to combine into a single methodology are the following:

1. that of Tzvetan Todorov, as illustrated in his *Grammaire du Décaméron*
2. that of Gérard Genette in *Narrative Discourse*
3. that of Roland Barthes in *S/Z*.

In each of these cases the critic has attempted to generate a method of analysis appropriate to the specific material under immediate consideration and to test the method on the material. But in every case, it is suggested, the method may have wider application as well. My thesis in this chapter is that all three of these methods do indeed have wider applications, that they complement one another in addressing the fictional text from different angles, and further, that they even suggest a sequence of use, each presenting itself as a segment in a metamethod in which they function as units of a syntagmatic process, units whose order should always be the same. The metamethod I wish to illustrate consists of approaching the text via Todorov, Genette, and Barthes, in that order. The illustration will be based upon a short story called "Eveline" from James Joyce's *Dubliners*.*

The three critics actually examine different levels or features of

---

*The text of "Eveline" is printed in full as an appendix to this chapter.

the text, though their work naturally overlaps at certain points. Todorov, who based his method on the hundred tales of Boccaccio's *Decameron*, calls his study a "grammar." Genette, who illustrates his system on Proust's *Recherche*, is interested in "figures" that operate at the "rhetorical" level of the text. Barthes, working with a novella of Balzac, is more completely semiotic, as he seeks to codify all the ways in which a fictional text generates its significations. These three writers, then, offer us a grammar, a rhetoric, and finally a semiotic of fiction. This is true—with certain qualifications, which will emerge from the following discussion.

Todorov's grammar has two main features. He reduces fictions to plot structures that can be represented by a simple symbolic logic, and he codes the semantic features of his symbolic notation so that they reveal the principal thematic concerns of the action in any story. Todorov's method calls for a summary of the story's action to be made first, and then for the reduction of the summary to symbolic form. But this procedure has two large faults. First, the summary must be intuitive, governed by no explicit system; and second, the resulting notation has a spurious exactitude, based upon its resemblance to the summary rather than to the fiction itself. Working with stories as simple and sharply delineated as Boccaccio's, the problem is not so great, but when we seek to move to modern fiction it becomes acute.

The critic of modern fictional texts must employ Todorov's approach as a heuristic tool, a way of focusing interpretation upon certain features of all fictional texts. Our perception of fictions as fictions depends in part upon our understanding of what Barthes calls the code of actions. We recognize a story as a story because we perceive in it a causal/chronological system that has, as Aristotle pointed out, a beginning, middle, and end. Todorov offers us a way of isolating the major action in any work of fiction so as to bring it to the foreground of our attention. Using his system of notation, we seek the story within any work of fiction. Obviously, most fictions are more than stories, especially modern fictions; and some fictions are antistories, pseudostories, in which the idea of story itself is parodied or denied for some ideological or thematic purpose. Todorov offers us a way to seek the story in any fiction and to record the results of that search. If we find no story, or a partial story, that, too, is a significant result.

But what *is* a story? Todorov will help us be precise in answering that question. A story is a certain kind of sequence of propositions. Fictional propositions are of two kinds: attributions and actions. The most fundamental fictional sequence is attribution, action, attribution—beginning, middle, end. Let me illustrate. If characters are nouns, attributes are adjectives, and actions are verbs, we can present a simple story in the following way:

$$X - A + (XA) \text{ opt} X \rightarrow Xa \rightarrow XA,$$

where

X = Boy
A = love, to be loved by someone
a = to seek love, to woo
optX = Boy (X) wishes (opt)
− = negation of attribute: −A is to lack love, to be unloved.

Thus the sequence reads Boy lacks love plus Boy wants to be loved which yields Boy seeks love which yields Boy is loved. We know this is a story because it is a sequence of propositions involving the same subject, in which the last proposition is a transformation of the first. An unhappy ending might be a simple repetition of the first proposition: X − A. A very unhappy ending might be X − A!, boy lacks love with a vengeance. But happy or unhappy, what makes the sequence a story is the return to the opening proposition at the end. Stories are about the successful or unsuccessful transformation of attributes.

In applying Todorov's method to modern stories, the first problem is often to isolate the major sequence of actions, to find the master story. "Eveline" is rather simple in this respect, but other stories in *Dubliners* are much more difficult. To find a story in "Ivy Day" is not so easy. But even "Eveline" presents problems of another sort. The chain of symbols representing the syntax of a story is just one aspect of its "grammar." The other aspect is lexical or semantic. We must reduce the complex of qualities associated with the characters (what Barthes calls the connotative code) to a few summary features that are activated by the story itself. This semantic summarizing is the most crucial aspect of the interpretive process at this level of analysis. In actual practice, the interpreter must simply try out attributions until they seem incapable of further refinement. The method here requires the skill of the interpreter, and it will display any lack of such skill mercilessly—but the method cannot provide it.

Here is a version of the story of "Eveline":

$$\begin{array}{ccccc} 1 & 2 & 3 & 4 & 5 \end{array}$$
$$XA + XB \to X - C + YaX + (X - A + X - B \to XC)\text{pred}X \to$$
$$\begin{array}{cccc} 6 & 7 & 8 & 9 \end{array}$$
$$(XbY)\text{pred}X + XA! \to X\text{not}bY \to (XB + X - C) \,!\, \text{imp}$$

X	Eveline
Y	Frank
A	a Dubliner
B	celibate
C	happy—respected, secure
a	to offer elopement
b	to accept elopement
−	negative of attribute
not	negative of verb
pred	predicts or expects
imp	is implied by discourse

The annotation may be read as follows: Eveline is a Dubliner—literally a resident of Dublin, but figuratively much more. This attribute is built up over the whole sequence of stories, is in fact what the stories are about, as the title of the book indicates. This story, like most of the others, marks most heavily such features as isolation, deprivation, and repression, combined with an inability to act so as to change this condition of life. Eveline is also celibate. Dubliners tend to be either celibate or unhappily married, and celibacy is usually marked in the stories as a negative attribute, connoting incompletion, frustration, isolation. The third proposition indicates that Eveline is unhappy with her life. This is less than explicit, but can be inferred from her reaction to Frank's proposal and other descriptions of her home life. The action of the story starts with Frank's proposal of elopement, which leads Eveline to imagine that her situation will change for the better, signified by the reversal of sign on the attributes in the fifth proposition. Her prediction of the elopement itself in the sixth proposition is in fact bound up with the changes she predicts in the fifth. All this is quite explicit in the text. But Eveline *is* a Dubliner! She finally refuses the elopement, and the story closes with the strong implication that her original condition resumes, only intensified by her having missed this chance to leave Dublin and change her life. This is a simple story, which could easily be coded as the negation of one of Vladimir Propp's Russian fairy tales. The prince comes to rescue the princess from the villain's dungeon, but she decides finally that the dungeon is less frightening than the thought of leaving it, and sends the hero home empty-handed. Naturalism sometimes generates its "authenticity" by the inversion of romance. But let us return to the process of notation and what it reveals.

Looking simply at the syntactic configuration here we see that the three attributive propositions which constitute the "situation" of "Eveline" are repeated with emphasis at or near the close of the narration. And though this repetition is more a matter of implication than of statement, the implications are quite clear. We can see also that the attributes remain unchanged: an essentially unhappy situation finally persists, even intensifies. This, in fact, is the rule of *Dubliners*. The grammar of these stories tends toward the persistence of unpleasant conditions—from bad to worse. A few stories show a change from better to worse. Only one shows any improvement of an opening situation, and that is "Two Gallants," in which the impecunious Lenehan is finally likely to benefit by sponging off his friend Corley, who has just received a gold coin from a servant girl in exchange for his sexual favors. But behind this "happy" ending the portrait of Lenehan as an aging sponger who is trapped in his Dublinesque existence becomes clearer and clearer. His real condition improves no more than Eveline's.

The point of this discussion is that Todorovian notation forces us to focus on questions of attribution, forces us to thematize the work. When applied to a body of works by a single author, such as the *Dubliners* stories, it brings to our attention recurrent features of syntactic and semantic coding, raising questions about such matters as why so many of these stories turn on celibacy and its various alternatives, and finally about the ultimate attribution, the state of being a Dubliner. This method is relatively crude, examining only two gross features of the text—action and attribution—but its usefulness for the analyst and the teacher is very real indeed.

The most elaborate and systematic apparatus yet developed for the study of fictional texts is that proposed by Gérard Genette in his *Narrative Discourse*. In the course of an extended discussion of Proust's *Recherche,* Genette presents a method for analyzing a fictional text according to its tense, mood, and voice—thus borrowing his terminology from the traditional grammar of the verb, on the grounds that all fiction can be seen as "the expansion of a verb." Genette begins by distinguishing three aspects of fictional texts that enable us to recognize them as fictional, and also provide us with points of departure for their study. Every fictional text comes to us in the form of a *récit* or narrative discourse—a text in fact. And this discourse informs us of a set of fictional events that can be distinguished from the text itself. Every fictional text conveys to us a story, which exists in a different spatiotemporal situation from the text itself, and from its own production or our reading of it. In addition to this, every narrative text also conveys explicitly or implicitly some circumstances of narrating, some explanation for its own existence as a text, both in relation to the events narrated and to some *narratee* or audience. When the narrative situation of a text is examined closely, the narrator and narratee virtually never correspond exactly with author and reader, nor do the circumstances of narration agree with those of a book's actual writing and reading.

Keeping in mind these three elements of all written fictions (the text, the narrating, and the story), Genette begins his study of narrative by examining aspects of what he calls fictional "tense." In the temporal arrangements of fiction he discerns three major areas for investigation: order, duration, and frequency. *Order* is the arrangement of events expressed as a relationship between story and text, the chronology of the story as opposed to the way the discourse arranges this chronology and presents it to us. (This is close to the Russian formalist distinction between story and plot.) *Duration* is a relationship between the temporal extension of events in the story and the attention devoted to them by the discourse. This is a matter of speed or velocity, which may be expressed as a ratio between the hours, days, and years of story time and the words and pages of the printed text. The third temporal aspect of a fictional text, *frequency,* involves the ways in which events may be repeated either in the story itself (the same thing happening more than once) or in the discourse (the same event described more than once).

Within these three main aspects of tense Genette makes many further discriminations, only some of which we will attend to here, as not all are significant for a study of "Eveline."

The order of presentation of the events in "Eveline" is both simple and complex. The base time of the narrative is the evening of Eveline's projected departure from Dublin. Joyce presents these events in two scenes: the first begins on page 105 (in the text appended to this chapter) with darkness falling as Eveline sits by her window, and ends with her standing up, on page 108. The second scene begins after the ellipsis dots on page 108. The time is that same night (though we must infer this) and the scene continues until the end of the story. Within this simple, chronological scheme, however, this story moves through an extraordinary complexity of temporal arrangement. Confining ourselves for the moment to fairly large and readily distinguishable blocks of time, we can discern a temporal movement in the story something like this, numbering these time blocks from 1 to 6:

A. Base time (beginning, into second paragraph) 5
B. Childhood (mid second par.) 1
C. Base time (end second par. and beginning of third) 5
D. (A complex section to be scrutinized more closely later on)
E. Recent past (Miss Gavan and the Stores) 4
F. Future ("her new home," p. 106) 6
G. Recent past (Saturday night, etc.) 4

H. Future ("She was about," p. 107) 6
 I. Recent past (Eveline's relationship with Frank) 4
 J. Earlier past (Frank's history) 2
K. Base time (p. 107—the "evening deepened") 5
L. Earlier past (Eveline's mother's illness and death) 3
M. Base time mixed with future (end of first section) 5/6
N. Ellipsis in base time 5
O. Base time (whole second scene, with only a hint of future) 5

Even ignoring many minor temporal shifts we can discern fifteen distinct sections ranging over at least six separate periods in the life of Eveline, extending from her childhood to her possible future with Frank. But because of the way that Joyce has handled the perspective of this story, all these times are contained within the base time of the two scenes. They are all presented to us as aspects of Eveline's thought in a base time which is very close to "present" tense, even though narrated in a conventional past. Even the ellipsis indicates a present and dramatic passage of time. Since Genette discusses perspective as an aspect of "mood," we shall return to it after examining more closely certain aspects of tense that we have thus far set aside.

The fourth temporal unit noted above is so complicated that I refrained from specifying its location in time. Now let us look at it more closely. The third section has brought us back to base time, with "Now" and "Home," as Eveline looks around her darkening room (105, last par.). Let us watch closely the temporal movement within a couple of sentences here:

> She looked [base time] around the room, reviewing [base time] all its familiar objects, which she had dusted [past, iterative] once a week for so many years, wondering [past, iterative] where on earth all the dust came from. Perhaps she would never see again [future, conditional, negative] those familiar objects from which she had never dreamed [past, negative, subordinated within future] of being divided [future, within past negative, within future].

What we have here is a rapid oscillation between the past seen as iterative, a familiar round of repeated events, dull but comforting, and a future dimly perceived as the absence of these familiar surroundings. The future as absence ("never see again") is a frightening prospect. Because she is trying to "weigh each side of the question" Eveline's thoughts continually move from the past to the future. But for her the future is at worst negative (never) and at best conditional: "she *would* be married. . . . People *would* treat her with respect then. She *would* not be treated as her mother had been" (106). And the future inevitably leads her back to the past. She can see it only dimly, negatively, conditionally. It has no reality for her, no more than Buenos Ayres as a place has more reality than the Melbourne of her father's "casual" expression. When she begins to think of herself as a wife, she fatally concludes by thinking of her mother. We should note in this respect that her future, if she should remain home, is a subject that eludes her even more completely than her future in Buenos Ayres, while she is weighing "each side of the question." We know that she has "palpitations" and we know that "latterly" her father has begun to threaten her with physical violence. And we can infer that her mother had been physically abused in the past. Eveline almost admits this thought to consciousness when she reflects that she would not be "treated as her mother had been" and then moves in the next sentence to thoughts of her father's violence (106, last par.). There is much in both the past and the future that is unexpressed in Eveline's revery.

In developing these considerations I have been led from thoughts of tense into questions of voice and perspective. As Genette points out, this kind of thing is inevitable in analysis, since we are arbitrarily dividing for discussion a thing that is indivisible, because we cannot hope to say everything about a text at once. But this analysis will take us even further into the concerns of the story if we let it. Time, as we are seeing, is not simply a feature of the structure of this narrative, it is a major element of Eveline's situation. "Her time was running out," the narrator tells us (108), and she knows it. She is facing a moment of terrible choice between a future she cannot conceive and one that she will not admit. Human beings are distinguished from other animals by their ability to project, to reach, through language and vision, into the future. But Eveline is so trapped in the past—in her promise to her dead mother, in the ritual of her church—that she not only fears the future but finally retreats from present awareness altogether: "Moving her lips in silent fervent prayer" (109/8–9), she has finally lost the gift of speech and all ability to perceive and communicate. She becomes "passive, like a helpless animal" (109/21).

Turning from the temporal order of a text to its duration, Genette distinguishes four basic speeds of narration:

1. The ellipsis–infinitely rapid
2. The summary–relatively rapid
3. The scene–relatively slow
4. The descriptive pause–zero degree of progress

The basic novelistic rhythm, he indicates, is an alternation between undramatic summaries that provide connections and dramatic scenes in which the decisive action takes place. In "Eveline" we have all four varieties of duration: an ellipsis between the two sections of the narrative; a summary of Eveline's and Frank's past lives; the dramatic scene at the quay; and even some description, though so little as to make virtually no pause in the story. But we need to notice some peculiar aspects of Joyce's employment of these techniques. First of all, he manages things so that all description and summarizing are presented as aspects of Eveline's thought, and hence function as drama or scene. The narrative segments set in base time do in fact constitute a scene of extended duration, in which a relatively short time in the story occupies a long part of the text. And the first scene, with all its temporal oscillation, gives us a sense of base time passing very slowly. Then the second scene, after the ellipsis, by stretching time out even more, emphasizes the passing of seconds, as the inexorable process of the ship's departure (time and tide wait for no man) brings the future and the present to a point of congruity, whereupon Eveline, no longer able to weigh past against future, is driven out of human time altogether into the frozen present of animal existence.

Genette's treatment of fictional mood also provides a useful way into Joyce's story. Genette divides mood into two aspects: distance and perspective. Narrative distance is a function of the amount and precision of detail provided in any text. The more detail given, the closer we come to scenic description. Some details may be presented gratuitously, as it were, to give "the effect of the real," of something named only because it is "really there." In

"Eveline" such items as the "odour of dusty cretonne," or the "coloured print of the promises made to Blessed Margaret Mary Alacoque" seem to function in this "gratuitous" way, as mere bits of "life." But in the hands of Joyce in particular, these informational bits are likely to carry meanings in more than one code. In this respect Genette's approach needs to be supplemented by that of Roland Barthes, as I shall suggest more extensively below.

In his discussion of distance and perspective Genette considers the critical debate on "showing" versus "telling" in fiction and the modernist emphasis on "showing," which he defines as a preference for scene over summary, with an attendant effacement of the narrator. Joyce, it is clear, is a perfect example of this tendency, at least in "Eveline," where scene reaches out to include all summary and where we have to exercise considerable ingenuity to detect a narrative persona manipulating Eveline's voice and perspective. Genette also insists on the analyst's observing a distinction between perspective and voice in critical study. The eyes we see through and the voice we hear are not necessarily the same in narrative, though in "Eveline" there seems to be little significant difference.

The various perspectives adoptable in fiction are matters of focus. Certain aspects of the events in any story may be clarified by the narrative focus, while others may be hidden or obscured, temporarily or permanently. Focus determines how far into the life of a character we may be allowed to penetrate, and how many characters will be open to interior scrutiny. "The type of focus is not fixed for a whole work, necessarily," Genette observes, "but for a determined segment of narrative which may be very brief." He develops a terminology for a number of varieties of perspective— internal, external, fixed, variable, multiple, and unfocused—but like their counterparts in American discussions of fictional point of view, these terms may not have sufficient analytical value to justify their taxonomic complexity. The shifts in narrative focus that really matter may function at a level where linguistic sensitivity and intuition count for more than apparatus. Even here, however, Genette gives us some interesting leads. He points to the tendency of fictions to employ strategies he calls "paralipse" and "paralepse": that is, the withholding from the reader of information which he "ought"—according to the prevailing focus—to receive; and the presenting to the reader of information that the prevailing level of focalization "ought" to render inaccessible. Joyce, it seems to me, is a highly paraleptic writer, in "Eveline" and in other works as well. In this story he chooses what Genette calls a fixed internal focus, all thoughts being filtered through the mind of Eveline herself, and presented in language much like her own in both syntax and diction (though this is technically a matter of voice rather than perspective—or rather *her* language is a matter of perspective, *his*, the narrator's, a matter of voice). In choosing Eveline as a focus, Joyce—as in many other stories—has selected a central intelligence who is not very intelligent. Here is where he differs most from both Proust and Henry James, who preferred an intelligence much like their own at the center of their work. (There are some exceptions to this, as in *What Maisie Knew,* but it can be argued that even Maisie is potentially a Jamesian intelligence, and she is certainly enveloped in a rich, Jamesian voice.) But Joyce favored, in the *Dubliners* stories, an internal perspective fixed in a mind that is not only deprived of certain knowledge about the events of the story but that is absolutely limited in education and intelligence. These limited minds trying to cope with painful situations, more than anything else, give the stories their ironic and naturalistic flavor. And this method posed for Joyce an esthetic problem that he delighted in solving—the problem of paralepse, of conveying to the reader more information than the code required by his perspective "ought" to convey.

Rhetorically speaking, whenever we encounter paralipse or paralepse we are in the presence of irony. In the case of "Eveline" we have already noted how Eveline suppresses certain thoughts about her future in Dublin, and the way in which she links associatively the ideas of her father's brutality and her mother's insanity and death without acknowledging the logical connection between them. In these instances Joyce is leading us to make inferences that result in our helping to "construct" the story we are reading. We, by an act of inference, piece together some of Eveline's situation, and at the same time are enabled to make the further inference that she is suppressing precisely the matter that we have inferred. This takes Joyce in the direction of what Roland Barthes calls the *"scriptible"* text, a modernist fiction that forces the reader to participate in the creation of its events and meanings. But I would argue that he stops well short of giving us liberty to construct what meanings we please. Our inferences are guided, unobtrusively but firmly, in ways that we have been investigating and will continue to investigate.

This discussion is taking us beyond the range of Genette's system of fictional analysis, but for a very good reason. His treatment of fictional voice, which is illuminating with respect to Proust, is simply not very helpful when we turn to Joyce, though Joyce is one of the most vocalic of writers. This is because Genette considers under voice only matters involving the relationship between distinguishable narrators and the tales they relate. Joyce's kind of ventriloqual effect, in which he narrates in the voice of a character while seeing the character as a third person, limiting himself to saying what the character might perceive but using this saying to convey the views of an invisible narrator—this possibility is just not sufficiently regarded by Genette, perhaps because it involves an interacting between perspective and voice, which he has been at such pains to separate. It is actually Roland Barthes who comes closest to offering us what we need to complete the analysis of a text like "Eveline."

In *S/Z*, his book-length analysis of Balzac's story "Sarrasine," Barthes works his way through the text, a few phrases or sentences at a time, interpreting these "lexias," as he calls them, according to the ways they generate meanings in five signifying systems or codes. His five codes are as follows:

1. The proairetic code or code of actions, which he calls "the main armature of the readerly text"—by which he means, among other things, all texts that are in fact narrative. Where most traditional critics, such as Aristotle and Todorov, would look only for major actions or plots, Barthes (in theory) sees all actions as codable, from the most trivial opening of a door to a romantic adventure. In practice, he applies some principles of selectivity. We recognize actions because we are able to name them. In most fiction (Barthes's readerly texts) we expect actions begun to be completed;

thus the principal action becomes the main armature of such a text. (Todorovian notation seeks to isolate this main armature for study.)

2. The hermeneutic code or code of puzzles plays on the reader's desire for "truth," for the answers to questions raised by the text. In examining "Sarrasine" Barthes names ten phases of hermeneutic coding, from the initial posing of a question or thematization of a subject that will become enigmatic, to the ultimate disclosure and decipherment of what has been withheld. Like the code of actions, the code of enigmas is a principal structuring agent of traditional narrative. Between the posing of a riddle and its solution in narrative, Barthes locates eight different ways of keeping the riddle alive without revealing its solution, including equivocations, snares, partial answers, and so forth. In certain kinds of fiction, such as detective stories, the hermeneutic code dominates the entire discourse. Together with the code of actions it is responsible for narrative suspense, for the reader's desire to complete, to finish the text.

3. The cultural codes. There are many of these. They constitute the text's references to things already "known" and codified by a culture. Barthes sees traditional realism as defined by its reference to what is already known. Flaubert's "Dictionary of Accepted Ideas" is a realist Bible. The axioms and proverbs of a culture or a subculture constitute already coded bits upon which novelists may rely. Balzac's work is heavily coded in this way.

4. The connotative codes. Under this rubric we find not one code but many. In reading, the reader "thematizes" the text. He notes that certain connotations of words and phrases in the text may be grouped with similar connotations of other words and phrases. As we recognize a "common nucleus" of connotations we locate a theme in the text. As clusters of connotation cling to a particular proper name we recognize a character with certain attributes. (It is worth noting that Barthes considers denotation as simply the "last" and strongest of connotations.)

5. The symbolic field. This is the aspect of fictional coding that is most specifically "structuralist"—or, more accurately, poststructuralist—in Barthes's presentation. It is based on the notion that meaning comes from some initial binary opposition or differentia-

tion—whether at the level of sounds becoming phonemes in the production of speech; or at the level of psychosexual opposition, through which a child learns that mother and father are different from each other and that this difference also makes the child the same as one of them and different from the other; or at the level of primitive cultural separation of the world into opposing forces or values that may be coded mythologically. In a verbal text this kind of symbolic opposition may be encoded in rhetorical figures such as antithesis, which is a privileged figure in Barthes's symbolic system.

Since the space and time for a Barthesian amble through the lexias of "Eveline" are not available, I shall invert his procedure and simply locate some elements of each code as found in Joyce's text.

1. CODE OF ACTIONS (PROAIRETIC)

In "Eveline" these range from the relatively trivial "She sat," completed four pages later by "She stood up," to the more consequential action of her leaving Dublin for good, which of course never occurs. This is a story of paralysis, which is a major connotative code in all the *Dubliners* stories. Significantly, we never see Eveline move a single step. Even in the last climactic scene her actions are described as "She stood.... She gripped.... She set her face." This increasing rigidity thematizes the connotative code of paralysis.

2. CODE OF ENIGMAS (HERMENEUTIC)

Joyce does not rely heavily on this code. Above all, he does not feel a need to complete it. We begin with some questions about who Eveline is, why she is tired, and the like, but there is no mystery about this. Frank is an enigma, of course. The discourse tells us something about him, but only gives us Eveline's thoughts about Frank's version of his life. There is also some mystery attached to Eveline's mother, the cause of her death, and the mysterious phrase she uttered which no one can decipher. But the discourse does not complete or "solve" these mysteries. Like the priest who went to Melbourne, they suggest a world not completely fathomable, beyond the comfortable realism of Balzacian discourse. The final enigma, the reason for Eveline's refusal, forces us back into the text, and out to the other *Dubliners* stories to find solutions that will never have the assurance of discursive "truth."

3. CULTURAL CODES

Cultural coding in this tale is not so much the property of any narrative voice, or of the discourse itself, as it is something in the minds of the characters. Eveline's father sees Frank under a code of cynical parental wisdom: "I know these sailor chaps." Eveline sees him as codified by romantic fiction: "Frank was very kind, manly, open-hearted." The discourse ratifies neither view. It avoids the cultural codes of Dublin, which so dominate the characters' lives. Of these, the most powerful is the code of Irish Catholicism, which would classify Eveline's action as a sin.

4. CONNOTATIVE CODES

The dominant connotative code is the code of paralysis, which is a major element in Eveline's character as well as in the world around her. It is connoted by Eveline's motionlessness throughout the story. It is even conveyed by the dreary, monotonous sentence structure—subject, verb, predicate, over and over again. And it is signified by such details as the promises made to Blessed Margaret Mary Alacoque, who was paralyzed until she vowed to dedicate herself to a religious life. The way in which this saintly lady's life comments on Eveline's own introduces another level of connotation, the ironic. Through its ironic combination of signs, the discourse paraleptically leads us to a view of Eveline's situation beyond her own perception of it. She sees herself as weighing evidence and deciding. But the discourse ironically indicates that she has no choice. She is already inscribed as a Dubliner in Joyce's code, and a Dubliner never decides, never escapes. As Diderot's *Jacques le fataliste* would have it, *il est écrit en haut,* it is written above—in Joyce's text.

5. THE SYMBOLIC CODE

For Joyce in *Dubliners* the primal opposition is not male versus female but sexed versus unsexed, usually presented as celibate versus profligate, an opposition that is almost unmediated by any linking term. Only the dead are fruitful or potent in Joyce's wasteland. In "Eveline," the sailor Frank is set in opposition to the father as a rival for Eveline, who is filling her mother's role in the household. In this symbolic opposition Frank is associated with water, freedom, the unknown, the future, and sexual potency. The father's house is dusty, Eveline is a slavey in it, but it is known, rooted in the past, and fruitless. As her father's slave/wife, Eveline will be sterile, impotent, celibate, a kind of nun, a Dubliner. This symbolic opposition emerges most powerfully from the clash of connotations in a single sentence in the final scene, when Eveline sees "the black mass of the boat, lying in beside the quay." This "black mass" is an innocent descriptive phrase which also connotes the sacrilegious power of the act Eveline is contemplating here. To board that boat, leave the land and enter upon the sea, would be to leave what is known, safe, already coded. It would be above all to flout the teachings of the church, to sin. The virgin, the nun, a celibate safely within the cultural codification of ritual is opposed to the defiled woman upon whose belly the black mass is blasphemously consummated. But look more closely. In that other harmless descriptive phrase, "lying in," another terror is connoted. To "lie in" is to be delivered of child, to be fruitful, to be uncelibate, not to play the mother's role for the father, but to displace her and the father both, sending them into the past. It is to accept life—and the danger of death. These connotations activate the symbolic level of the text by their juxtaposition of its antitheses. And in that extraordinary figure, "All the seas of the world tumbled about her heart," the discourse connotes both the heart surrounded by amniotic fluid ready to burst with life, and also the fear of drowning in life itself, lured beyond her depth by a person she can no longer allow herself to recognize.

Our final vision of Eveline is of a creature in a state of symbolic deprivation. If the symbolic code is rooted in the fundamental processes of cognition and articulation, what is signified in that code at the end of "Eveline" is a creature who has lost those fundamental processes, not only at the level of speech and language but even the more fundamental semiotic functions of gesture and facial signals: "She set her white face to him, passive, like a helpless animal. Her eyes gave him no sign of love or farewell or recognition." However we interpret the story, we are surely intended to regard with pity and fear the situation of this young woman absolutely incommunicado, capable of giving "no sign."

EVELINE
by James Joyce

She sat at the window watching the evening invade the avenue. Her head was leaned against the window curtains and in her nostrils was the odour of dusty cretonne. She was tired.

Few people passed. The man out of the last house passed on his way home; she heard his footsteps clacking along the concrete pavement and afterwards crunching on the cinder path before the new red houses. One time there used to be a field there in which they used to play every evening with other people's children. Then the man from Belfast bought the field and built houses in it—not like their little brown houses but bright brick houses with shining roofs. The children of the avenue used to play together in that field—the Devines, the Waters, the Dunns, little Keogh the cripple, she and her brothers and sisters. Ernest, however, never played: he was too grown up. Her father used often to hunt them in out of the field with his blackthorn stick; but usually little Keogh used to keep *nix* and call out when he saw her father coming. Still they seemed to have been rather happy then. Her father was not so bad then; and besides, her mother was alive. That was a long time ago; she and her brothers and sisters were all grown up; her mother was dead. Tizzie Dunn was dead, too, and the Waters had gone back to England. Everything changes. Now she was going to go away like the others, to leave her home.

Home! She looked around the room, reviewing all its familiar objects which she had dusted once a week for so many years, wondering where on earth all the dust came from. Perhaps she would never see again those familiar objects from which she had never dreamed of being divided. And yet during all those years she had never found out the name of the priest whose yellowing photograph hung on the wall above the broken harmonium beside the coloured print of the promises made to Blessed Margaret Mary Alacoque. He had been a school friend of her father. Whenever he showed the photograph to a visitor her father used to pass it with a casual word:

—He is in Melbourne now.

She had consented to go away, to leave her home. Was that wise? She tried to weigh each side of the question. In her home anyway she had shelter and food; she had those whom she had known all her life about her. Of course she had to work hard both in the house and at business. What would they say of her in the Stores when they found out that she had run away with a fellow? Say she was a fool, perhaps; and her place would be filled up by advertisement. Miss Gavan would be glad. She had always had an edge on her, especially whenever there were people listening.

—Miss Hill, don't you see these ladies are waiting?

—Look lively, Miss Hill, please.

She would not cry many tears at leaving the Stores.

But in her new home, in a distant unknown country, it would not be like that. Then she would be married—she, Eveline. People would treat her with respect then. She would not be treated as her mother had been. Even now, though she was over nineteen, she sometimes felt herself in danger of her father's violence. She knew it was that that had given her the palpitations. When they were growing up he had never gone for her, like he used to go for Harry and Ernest, because she was a girl; but latterly he had begun to threaten her and say what he would do to her only for her dead mother's sake. And now she had nobody to protect her. Ernest was dead and Harry, who was in the church decorating business, was nearly always down somewhere in the country. Besides, the invariable squabble for money on Saturday nights had begun to weary her unspeakably. She always gave her entire wages—seven shillings—and Harry always sent up what he could but the trouble was to get any money from her father. He said she used to squander the money, that she had no head, that he wasn't going to give her his hard-earned money to throw about the streets, and much more, for he was usually fairly bad of a Saturday night. In the end he would give her the money and ask her had she any intention of buying Sunday's dinner. Then she had to rush out as quickly as she could and do her marketing, holding her black leather purse tightly in her hand as she elbowed her way through the crowds and returning home late under her load of provisions. She had hard work to keep the house together and to see that the two young children who had been left to her charge went to school regularly and got their meals regularly. It was hard work—a hard life—but now that she was about to leave it she did not find it a wholly undesirable life.

She was about to explore another life with Frank. Frank was very kind, manly, open-hearted. She was to go away with him by the night-boat to be his wife and to live with him in Buenos Ayres where he had a home waiting for her. How well she remembered the first time she had seen him; he was lodging in a house on the main road where she used to visit. It seemed a few weeks ago. He was standing at the gate, his peaked cap pushed back on his head and his hair tumbled forward over a face of bronze. Then they had come to know each other. He used to meet her outside the Stores every evening and see her home. He took her to see *The Bohemian Girl* and she felt elated as she sat in an unaccustomed part of the theatre with him. He was awfully fond of music and sang a little. People knew that they were courting and, when he sang about the lass that loves a sailor, she always felt pleasantly confused. He used to call her Poppens out of fun. First of all it had been an excitement for her to have a fellow and then she had begun to like him. He had tales of distant countries. He had started as a deck boy at a pound a month on a ship of the Allan Line going out to Canada. He told her the names of the ships he had been on and the names of the different services. He had sailed through the Straits of Magellan and he told her stories of the terrible Patagonians. He had fallen on his feet in Buenos Ayres, he said, and had come over to the old country just for a holiday. Of course, her father had found out the affair and had forbidden her to have anything to say to him.

—I know these sailor chaps, he said.

One day he had quarrelled with Frank and after that she had to meet her lover secretly.

The evening deepened in the avenue. The white of two letters in her lap grew indistinct. One was to Harry; the other was to her father. Ernest had been her favourite but she liked Harry too. Her father was becoming old lately, she noticed; he would miss her. Sometimes he could be very nice. Not long before, when she had been laid up for a day, he had read her out a ghost story and made toast for her at the fire. Another day, when their mother was alive, they had all gone for a picnic to the Hill of Howth. She remembered her father putting on her mother's bonnet to make the children laugh.

Her time was running out but she continued to sit by the window, leaning her head against the window curtain, inhaling the odour of dusty cretonne. Down far in the avenue she could hear a street organ playing. She knew the air. Strange that it should come that very night to remind her of the promise to her mother, her promise to keep the home together as long as she could. She remembered the last night of her mother's illness; she was again in the close dark room at the other side of the hall and outside she heard a melancholy air of Italy. The organ-player had been ordered to go away and given sixpence. She remembered her father strutting back into the sickroom saying:

—Damned Italians! coming over here!

As she mused the pitiful vision of her mother's life laid its spell on the very quick of her being—that life of commonplace sacrifices closing in final craziness. She trembled as she heard her mother's voice saying constantly with foolish insistence:

—Derevaun Seraun! Derevaun Seraun!

She stood up in a sudden impulse of terror. Escape! She must escape! Frank would save her. He would give her life, perhaps love, too. But she wanted to live. Why should she be unhappy? She had a right to happiness. Frank would take her in his arms, fold her in his arms. He would save her.

.   .   .   .

She stood among the swaying crowd in the station at the North Wall. He held her hand and she knew that he was speaking to her, saying something about the passage over and over again. The station was full of soldiers with brown baggages. Through the wide doors of the sheds she caught a glimpse of the black mass of the boat, lying in beside the quay wall, with illumined portholes. She answered nothing. She felt her cheek pale and cold and, out of a maze of distress, she prayed to God to direct her, to show her what was her duty. The boat blew a long mournful whistle into the mist. If she went, to-morrow she would be on the sea with Frank, steaming towards Buenos Ayres. Their passage had been booked. Could she still draw back after all he had done for her? Her distress awoke a nausea in her body and she kept moving her lips in silent fervent prayer.

A bell clanged upon her heart. She felt him seize her hand:
—Come!

All the seas of the world tumbled about her heart. He was drawing her into them: he would drown her. She gripped with both hands at the iron railing.
—Come!

No! No! No! It was impossible. Her hands clutched the iron in frenzy. Amid the seas she sent a cry of anguish!
—Eveline! Evvy!

He rushed beyond the barrier and called to her to follow. He was shouted at to go on but he still called to her. She set her white face to him, passive, like a helpless animal. Her eyes gave him no sign of love or farewell or recognition.

7

DECODING PAPA: "A VERY SHORT STORY" AS WORK AND TEXT *

The semiotic study of a literary text is not wholly unlike traditional interpretation or rhetorical analysis, nor is it meant to replace these other modes of response to literary works. But the semiotic critic situates the text somewhat differently, privileges different dimensions of the text, and uses a critical methodology adapted to the semiotic enterprise. Most interpretive methods privilege the "meaning" of the text. Hermeneutic critics seek authorial or intentional meaning; the New Critics seek the ambiguities of "textual" meaning; the "reader response" critics allow readers to make meaning. With respect to meaning the semiotic critic is situated differently. Such a critic looks for the generic or discursive structures that enable and constrain meaning.

Under semiotic inspection neither the author nor the reader is free to make meaning. Regardless of their lives as individuals, as author and reader they are traversed by codes that enable their communicative adventures at the cost of setting limits to the messages they can exchange. A literary text, then, is not simply a set of words, but (as Roland Barthes demonstrated in *S/Z*, though not necessarily in just that way) a network of codes that enables the marks on the page to be read as a text of a particular sort.

In decoding narrative texts, the semiotic method is based on two simple but powerful analytical tools: the distinction between story

*Because of the author's restrictions against reprinting "A Very Short Story" as a whole in any work other than a volume made up exclusively of his own work, the full text of the story has not been included here. The reader is requested to consult the text of "A Very Short Story" in Hemingway's *In Our Time* or *The Short Stories of Ernest Hemingway,* New York: Charles Scribner's Sons (The Scribner Library), before reading this chapter. My apologies for the inconvenience.

and discourse, on the one hand, and that between text and events on the other. The distinction between story and discourse is grounded in a linguistic observation by Emile Benveniste to the effect that some languages (notably French and Greek) have a special tense of the verb used for the narration of past events. (See "The Correlations of Tense in the French Verb," chapter 19 of *Problems in General Linguistics*. See also Seymour Chatman, *Story and Discourse*.) This tense, the aorist or *passé simple*, emphasizes the relationship between the utterance and the situation the utterance refers to, between the narration and the events narrated. This is *par excellence* the mode of written transcriptions of events: *histoire* or "story." Benveniste contrasts this with the mode of *discours* or "discourse," in which the present contact between speaker and listener is emphasized. Discourse is rhetorical, and related to oral persuasion. Story is referential and related to written documentation. Discourse is now; story is then. Story speaks of he and she; discourse is a matter of you and me, I and thou.

In any fictional text, then, we can discern certain features that are of the story: reports on actions, mentions of times and places, and the like. We can also find elements that are of the discourse: evaluations, reflections, language that suggests an authorial or at least narratorial presence who is addressing a reader or narratee with a persuasive aim in mind. When we are told that someone "smiled cruelly," we can detect more of story in the verb and more of discourse in the adverb. Some fictional texts, those of D. H. Lawrence for example, are highly discursive. To read a Lawrence story is to enter into a personal realtionship with someone who resembles the writer of Lawrence's private correspondence. Hemingway, on the other hand, often seems to have made a strong effort to eliminate discourse altogether—an effort that is apparent in "A Very Short Story."

The distinction between story and discourse is closely related to another with which it is sometimes confused, and that is the distinction between the *récit* and *diégésis* of a narrative. In this case we are meant to distinguish between the whole text of a narration as a text, on the one hand, and the events narrated as events on the other. We can take over the Greek term, diegesis, for the system of characters and events, and simply anglicize the other term as recital; or just refer to the "text" when we mean the words and the "diegesis" for what they encourage us to create as a fiction.

The text itself may be analyzed into components of story and discourse, but it may also be considered in relation to the diegesis. One of the primary qualities of those texts we understand as fiction is that they generate a diegetic order that has an astonishing independence from its text. To put it simply, once a story is told it can be recreated in a recognizable way by a totally new set of words—in another language, for instance—or in another medium altogether. The implications of this for analysis are profound. Let us explore some of them.

A fictional diegesis draws its nourishment not simply from the words of its text but from its immediate culture and its literary tradition. The magical words "once upon a time" in English set in motion a machine of considerable momentum which can hardly be turned off without the equally magical "they lived happily ever after" or some near equivalent. The diegetic processes of "realistic" narrative are no less insistent. "A Very Short Story," by its location in Hemingway's larger text (*In Our Time*), and a few key words—Padua, carried, searchlights, duty, operating, front, armistice—allows us to supply the crucial notions of military hospital, nurse, soldier, and World War I that the diegesis requires.

This process is so crucial that we should perhaps stop and explore its implications. The words on the page are not the story. The text is not the diegesis. The story is constructed by the reader from the words on the page by an inferential process—a skill that can be developed. The reader's role is in a sense creative—without it, no story exists—but it is also constrained by rules of inference that set limits to the legitimacy of the reader's constructions. Any interpretive dispute may be properly brought back to the "words on the page," of course, but these words never speak their own meaning. The essence of writing, as opposed to speech, is that the reader speaks the written words, the words that the writer has abandoned. A keen sense of this situation motivates the various sorts of "envoi" that writers supplied for their books in the early days of printing. They felt that their books were mute and would be spoken by others.

In reading a narrative, then, we translate a text into a diegisis according to codes we have internalized. This is simply the narrative version of the normal reading process. As E. D. Hirsch has recently reminded us (in the *Philosophy of Composition* [Chicago, 1977], pp. 122–23), for almost a century research in reading (Binet and Henri in 1894, Fillenbaum in 1966, Sachs in 1967, Johnson-Laird in 1970, Levelt and Kampen in 1975, and Brewer in 1975—specific citations can be found in Hirsch) has shown us that memory stores not the words of texts but their concepts, not the signifiers but the signifieds. When we read a narrative text, then, we process it as a diegesis. If we retell the story, it will be in our own words. To the extent that the distinction between poetry and fiction is a useful one, it is based on the notion of poetry as monumental, fixed in the words of the text and therefore untranslatable; while fiction has proved highly translatable because its essence is not in its language but in its diegetic structure. As fiction approaches the condition of poetry, its precise words become more important; as poetry moves toward narrative, its specific language decreases in importance.

In reading fiction, then, we actually translate from the text to a diegesis, substituting narrative units (characters, scenes, events, and so on) for verbal units (nouns, adjectives, phrases, clauses, etc.). And we perform other changes as well. We organize the material we receive so as to make it memorable, which means that we systematize it as much as possible. In the diegetic system we construct, time flows at a uniform rate; events occur in chronological order; people and places have the qualities expected of them—unless the text specifies otherwise. A writer may relocate the Eiffel Tower to Chicago but unless we are told this we will assume that a scene below that tower takes place in Paris—a Paris equipped with all the other items accorded it in our cultural paradigm.

Places and other entities with recognizable proper names (Napoleon, Waterloo, Broadway) enter the diegesis coded by culture. The events reported in a narrative text, however, will be stored in accordance with a syntactic code based on a chronological structure. The text may present the events that compose a story in any order, plunging *in medias res* or following through from beginning to end, but the diegesis always seeks to arrange them in chronological sequence. The text may expand a minute into pages or cram years into a single sentence, for its own ends, but the minutes and years remain minutes and years of diegetic time all the same. In short, the text may discuss what it chooses, but once a diegesis is set in motion no text can ever completely control it. "How many children had Lady Macbeth?" is not simply the query of a naive interpreter but the expression of a normal diegetic impulse. Where authors and texts delight in equivocation, the reader needs certainty and closure to complete the diegetic processing of textual materials. From this conflict of interests comes a tension that many modern writers exploit.

The semiotician takes the reader's diegetic impulse and establishes it as a principle of structuration. The logic of diegetic structure provides a norm, a benchmark for the study of textual strategies, enabling us to explore the dialogue between text and diegesis, looking for points of stress, where the text changes its ways in order to control the diegetic material for its own ends. The keys to both affect and intention may be found at these points. Does the text return obsessively to one episode of diegetic history? Does it disturb diegetic order to tell about something important to its own discursive ends? Does it omit something that diegetic inertia deems important? Does it change its viewpoint on diegetic events? Does it conceal things? Does it force evaluations through the rhetoric of its discourse? The calm inertia of diegetic process, moved by the weight of culture and tradition and the needs of memory itself, offers a stable background for the mapping of textual strategies. And our most esthetically ambitious texts will be those that find it most necessary to put their own stamp on the diegetic process.

Hemingway's "A Very Short Story" presents itself as exceptionally reticent. The familiar Hemingway style, which Gérard Genette has called "behaviorist," seems to efface itself, to offer us a pure diegesis. Boy meets girl—a "cute meet," as they used to say in Hollywood—they fall in love, become lovers, plan to marry, but the vicissitudes of war separate them, and finally forces that are too strong for them bring about their defeat. This is the story, is it not: a quasi-naturalistic slice of life that begins almost like a fairy tale ("Once upon a time in another country . . ."—and ends with the ne-

gation of the fairy-tale formula ("and they lived unhappily ever
after")—a negation that proclaims the text's realistic or naturalistic status? But there is already a tension here, between the open
form of the slice of life and the neat closure of the fairy tale, which
emerges most clearly if we compare the progress of diegetic time
with the movement of the text. We can do this in a crude way by
mapping the hours, days, and weeks of diegetic time against the
paragraphs of the text. The slowest paragraphs are the first: one
night; and the third: one trip to the Duomo. The fastest are the
fourth: his time at the front; the sixth: Luz's time in Pordenone;
and the seventh or last: which carries Luz to the point of infinity
with the word "never." The narrative thus increases its speed
throughout, and achieves its effect of culmination by the use of the
infinite terms in the last paragraph. The text might easily have con-
tented itself with recounting the fact that the major did not marry
Luz in the spring, but it feels obliged to add "or any other time,"
just as it is obliged to use the word "never" in the next sentence.
Something punitive is going on here, as the discourse seems to be
revenging itself upon the character. Why?

Before trying to answer that question we would do well to consider some other features of the text/diegesis relationship. From
the first paragraph on, it is noticeable that one of the two main
characters in the diegesis has a name in the text while the other is
always referred to by a pronoun. Why should this be? The answer
emerges when we correlate this detail with other features of the
text/diegesis relationship. The text, as we have observed, is reticent, as if it, too, does not want to "blab about anything during the
silly, talky time." But it is more reticent about some things than
others. In the first paragraph, the male character is introduced in
the first sentence. Luz appears in the fifth. When she sits on the bed
we are told, "she was cool and fresh in the hot night." Why this
information about her temperature? She is the nurse, after all, and
he the patient. In fact it is not information about how she feels at
all, but about how she appears to him. The text is completely reticent about how he feels himself, though the implication is that he
finds her coolness attractive. How he seems to her or how she feels
about him are not considered relevant. This is a selective reticence. Our vision is subjectively with him (as the personal pronoun

implies), while Luz is seen more objectively (as the proper name implies). The final implication of paragraph 1 is that they make love right then and there. But the reticent text makes the reader responsible for closing that little gap in the diegesis.

This matter of the point of view taken by the text can be established more clearly with the use of a sort of litmus test developed by Roland Barthes. If we rewrite the text substituting the first-person pronoun for the third, we can tell whether or not we are dealing with what Barthes calls a "personal system," a covert, first-person narration (see "Introduction to the Structural Analysis of Narratives," in *Image-Music-Text,* p. 112). In the case of "A Very Short Story," where we have two third-person characters of apparently equal consequence, we must rewrite the story twice to find out what we need to know. Actually, the issue is settled conclusively after the first two paragraphs, which are all I will present here:

The first two paragraphs of "A Very Short Story" rewritten—"he" transposed to "I":

> One hot evening in Padua they carried me up onto the roof and I could look out over the top of the town. There were chimney swifts in the sky. After a while it got dark and the searchlights came out. The others went down and took the bottle with them. Luz and I could hear them below on the balcony. Luz sat on the bed. She was cool and fresh in the hot night.
>
> Luz stayed on night duty for three months. They were glad to let her. When they operated on me she prepared me for the operating table; and we had a joke about friend or enema. I went under the anaesthetic holding tight on to myself so I would not blab about anything during the silly, talky time. After I got on crutches I used to take the temperatures so Luz would not have to get up from the bed. There were only a few patients, and they all knew about it. They all liked Luz. As I walked back along the halls I thought of Luz in my bed.

The same paragraphs—"Luz" transposed to "I":

> One hot evening in Padua they carried him up onto the roof and he could look out over the top of the town. There were chimney swifts in the sky. After a while it got dark and the searchlights came out. The others went down and took the bottles with them. He and I could hear

them below on the balcony. I sat on the bed. I was cool and fresh in the hot night.

I stayed on night duty for three months. They were glad to let me. When they operated on him I prepared him for the operating table; and we had a joke about friend or enema. He went under the anaesthetic holding tight on to himself so he would not blab about anything during the silly, talky time. After he got on crutches he used to take the temperatures so I would not have to get up from the bed. There were only a few patients, and they all knew about it. They all liked me. As he walked back along the halls he thought of me in his bed.

"He" transposes to "I" perfectly, but "Luz" does not. In the second rewriting the first person itself enters the discourse with a shocking abruptness, since the earlier sentences seem to have been from the male patient's point of view. The stress becomes greater in the last sentence of the first paragraph, which has been constructed to indicate how she appeared to him, not how she seemed to herself. But the last two sentences of the second paragraph in the second rewriting are even more ludicrous, with the first-person narrator informing us of how well liked she was, and finally describing his thoughts about her. In this rewriting there is simply too great a tension between the angle of vision and the person of the voice. The discourse loses its coherence. But the first rewriting is completely coherent because in it voice and vision coincide. It is really his narrative all the way. The third-person narration of the original text is a disguise, a mask of pseudo-objectivity worn by the text for its own rhetorical purposes.

The discourse of this text, as I have suggested, is marked by its reticence, but this reticence of the text is contrasted with a certain amount of talkativeness in the diegesis. He, of course, doesn't want to "blab," but *they* want "every one to know about" their relationship. Implication: *she* is the one who wants the news spread. There is absolutely no direct discourse in the text, but there are two paragraphs devoted to letters and one to recounting a quarrel. Here, too, we find reticence juxtaposed to talkativeness. Luz writes many letters to him while he is at the front. But the text does not say whether he wrote any to her. Hers are clearly repetitive and hyperbolic. The style of the discourse becomes unusually paratactic—even for Hemingway—whenever her letters are presented. "They were all about the hospital, *and how* much she loved him *and how* it was impossible to get along without him *and how* terrible it was missing him at night" (my italics). The repetitive "how"s, the hyperbolic "impossible" and "terrible," and all the "and"s suggest an unfortunate prose style even without direct quotation. Above all, they indicate an ominous lack of reticence.

The quarrel is not represented in the text but the "agreement" that causes it is summarized for us, at least in part. It takes the form of a series of conditions that *he* must fulfill in order to be rewarded with Luz's hand in marraige. Curiously, the conditions are represented not only as things it is "understood" that he will and will not do but also as things he wants and does not want to do. He does not "want to see his friends or any one in the States. Only to get a job and be married." It is not difficult to imagine a man being willing to avoid his friends, to work, and to stay sober in order to please a woman, but it is hard to imagine any human being who does not "*want* to see his friends or *anyone*." Not *want* to? Not *anyone*? The text seems to be reporting on the diegesis in a most curious way here. This is not simply reticence but irony. There is a strong implication that he is being coerced, pushed too far, even having his masculinity abused. If there are any conditions laid upon Luz, we do not hear of them.

Finally, the final letter arrives. In reporting it the text clearly allows Luz's prose to shine through once again, complete with repetition of the horrible phrase about the "boy and girl" quality of their relationship and the splendidly hyperbolic cacophony of "expected, absolutely unexpectedly." Her behavior belies her words. Her true awfulness, amply suggested earlier by the reticent text, blazes forth here as her hideous discourse perfectly complements her treacherous behavior.

But how did *he* behave while she was discovering the glories of Latin love? *Nihil dixit.* The text maintains what we can now clearly see as a specifically manly reticence. Did he drink? Did he see his friends? Or anyone? Did he want to? We know not. We do know, however, of his vehicular indiscretion in Lincoln Park and its result. The text is too generous and manly to say so, of course, but we know that this, too, is Luz's fault. She wounded him in the heart and "a short time after" this salesgirl got him in an even more vital place. The discourse leaves them both unhappy, but it clearly makes Luz the agent of the unhappiness.

And what does it make him? Why, the patient, of course. He is always being carried about, given enemas, operated on, sent to the front, sent home, not wanting anything, reading letters. He is wounded at the beginning and wounded at the end. The all-American victim: polite, reticent, and just waiting for an accident to happen to him. Who is to blame if his accidents keep taking the form of women? Who indeed? Whose discourse is this, whose story, whose diegesis, whose world? It is Papa's, for course, who taught a whole generation of male readers to prepare for a world where men may be your friends but women are surely the enema.

The story quite literally leaves its protagonist wounded in his sex by contact with a woman. From the bed in Padua to the back seat in Lincoln Park our Hero is carried from wound to wound. We never hear the accents of his voice or the intonations of his prose. We do not have to. The text speaks for him. Its voice is his. And its reticence is his as well. In this connection we should look once again at a passage in the second paragraph: "...they had a joke about friend or enema. He went under the anaesthetic holding tight on to himself so he would not..." Up to this point in the second sentence we are not aware that there has been a change of topic from that which closed the earlier sentence. The language of oral retentiveness coincides neatly with that of anal retentiveness. Logorrhea and diarrhea are equally embarrassing. Enemas are enemies and to "blab about anything during the silly, talky time" (to finish the sentence) would be as bad as to discharge matter freely from the opposite end of the alimentary canal. As Hemingway put it on another occasion: "If you talk about it, you lose it."

The point of this discussion is that the text reveals the principle behind its reticent prose style through an impartial and equal distress at the idea of excessive discharge of either verbal or fecal matter. It is an anal retentive style, then, in a surprisingly literal way. And through this style the text presents us with a lesson about women. Luz first gives our retentive hero a literal enema and then she metaphorically emasculates him by making him renounce alcohol, friends, and all the pleasures of life. The salesgirl from the loop merely administers the literal coup de grace to his already figuratively damaged sexuality.

Having come this far with a semiotic analysis, we can begin to distinguish it more precisely from New Critical exegesis. In doing so, we must begin by admitting that the two appraoches share a certain number of interpretive gestures. We must also recognize that no two semiotic analyses or New Critical exegeses are likely to be identical. The major differences in the two critical approaches can be traced to their different conceptions of the object of study: for New Criticism, the work; for semiotics, the text. As a work, "A Very Short Story" must be seen as complete, unified, shaped into an aesthetic object, a verbal icon. The pedagogical implications of this are important.

The student interpreting "A Very Short Story" as a "work" is put into an interesting position. Like many of Hemingway's early stories, this one presents a male character favorably and a female unfavorably. In fact, it strongly implies favorable things about masculinity and unfavorable things about feminity. It does this, as our semiotic analysis has shown, by mapping certain traits on to a value structure. The good, loyal, reticent male character is supported by the discourse, through its covert first-person perspective and the complicity of its style with those values. The bad, treacherous, talkative female is cast out. Even the carefully established point of view is violated in the last paragraph so that the narrator can track Luz through eternity and assure us that she never married her major "in the spring, or any other time." But for the most part Hemingway's control over his text is so great that the anger at the root of the story is transformed into what we may take as the cool, lapidary prose of the pure, impersonal artist.

And there definitely is an anger behind this story, to which we shall soon turn our attention. For the moment we must follow a bit further the situation of the student faced with this story in the form of a "work" to be interpreted. The concept of "the student" is one of those transcendental abstractions that we accept for convenience's sake and often come to regret. We can begin to break it down by reminding ourselves that students come in at least two genders. Actual students read this story in different ways. Most male students sympathize with the protagonist and are very critical of Luz—as, indeed, the discourse asks them to be. Many female students try to read the story as sympathetic to Luz, blaming events on the "weakness" of the young man or the state of the world. This is a possible interpretation, but it is not well supported by the text. Thus the female student must either "misread" the work (that is, she must offer the more weakly supported of two interpretations) or accept one more blow to her self-esteem as a woman. Faced with this story in a competitive classroom, women are put at a disadvantage. They are, in fact, in a double bind.

By New Critical standards the narrator is impersonal and reliable. The words on the page are all we have, and they tell us of a garrulous, faithless woman who was unworthy of the love of a loyal young man. But semiotic analysis has already suggested alternatives to this view. Seen as a text that presents a diegesis, this story is far from complete. There are gaps in the diegesis, reticences in the text, and a highly manipulative use of covert first-person narrative. There are signs of anger and vengefulness in the text, too, that suggest not an omniscient impersonal author but a partial, flawed human being—like the rest of us—behind the words on the page.

As a text, this story refers to other texts: to the fairy tale it is so definitely not, to other stories of betrayal (like *Troilus and Criseyde,* in which the Greek Diomedes plays the part of the Italian major), and to the other stories that surrounded it in Hemingway's *In Our Time.* But it also must be seen as a text among a particular set of other texts by Hemingway that present very similar diegetic material. These are, in chronological order, a manuscript called "Personal" (Young and Mann, *The Hemingway Manuscripts* [University Park, Penn., 1969], 11C), "chapter 10" in *in our time* (Paris, 1924), and various drafts of a novel that was finally published as *A Farewell to Arms* in 1929. All of these texts generate diegeses centered on a nurse in an Italian hospital. From Hemingway's letters and various other texts, including reports of interviews with the principals, yet another diegesis can be generated. In this one, a nineteen-year-old American Red Cross worker named Ernest Hemingway meets a Red Cross nurse named Agnes Hannah von Kurowsky, a twenty-six-year-old American woman, at a hospital in Milan, and falls in love with her. She calls him Kid and he calls her Mrs. Kid. When she volunteers for service in Florence during an influenza outbreak, he writes her many letters. ("He wrote to her daily, sometimes twice a day. She answered as often as her duties would allow." Carlos Baker, *Ernest Hemingway* [New York, 1980], p. 71.) They continue to correspond when she moves to Treviso near Padua to help out during another epidemic. He travels around in Italy, but his wounds prevent him from returning to the front. He sees Agnes a few more times before leaving Italy for the States.

He describes one of these visits in a letter to his friend, Bill Smith:

> But listen what kind of a girl I have: Lately I've been hitting it up—about 18 martinis a day and 4 days ago I left the hospital and hopped camions 200 miles up to the Front A.W.O.L. to visit some pals. Ossifers in the R.G.A. British outside of Padova. Their batteries are en repose. They gave me a wonderful time and we used the staff car and I rode to the hounds on the Colonels charger. Leg and all.
>
> But Bill to continue. We went in the staff car up to TREVISO where the missus [Agnes von Kurowsky] is in a Field Hospital. She had heard about my hitting the alcohol and did she lecture me? She did not.
>
> She said, "Kid we're going to be partners. So if you are going to drink I am too. Just the same amount." And she'd gotten some damn whiskey and poured some of the raw stuff out and she'd never had a drink of anything before except wine and I know what she thinks of booze. And William that brought me up shortly. Bill this is some girl and I thank God I got crucked so I met her. Damn it I really honestly can't see what the devil she can see in the brutal Stein but by some very lucky astigmatism she loves me Bill. So I'm going to hit the States and start working for the Firm. Ag says we can have a wonderful time being poor together and having been poor alone for some years and always more or less happy I think it can be managed.
>
> So now all I have to do is hit the minimum living wage for two and lay up enough for six weeks or so up North and call on you for service as a best man. Why man I've only got about 50 more years to live and I don't want to waste any of them and every minute that I'm away from that Kid is wasted. [Carlos Baker, ed. *Ernest Hemingway, Selected Letters 1917–1961*, New York, 1981, p. 20]

When Ernest leaves Italy from Genoa in January 1919, the romance is still sexually unconsummated (according to Agnes von

Kurowsky herself and the best judgment of Michael Reynolds, who reports this in *Hemingway's First War* [Princeton, 1976] and Carlos Baker, who discusses these events in *Ernest Hemingway, A Life Story* [New York, 1969].) Hemingway in fact goes home believing that when he gets established in a job that will support two people, Agnes will return and marry him. What she believed at that time cannot be determined.

At home Ernest saw many of his friends and partied a good deal. After one of these parties in his parents' home the unconscious bodies of two friends were stumbled over by Ernest and his older sister as they closed up the house. They agreed that the "Italian celebrations had gone too far." He still did not have a regular job when a letter from Agnes arrived in March of 1919. This is the way his sister Marcelline describes the event:

> For days Ernie had been watching the mails. He was irritable and on edge with the waiting. Then the letter came. After he read it he went to bed and was actually ill. We didn't know what was the matter with Ernie at first. He did not respond to medical treatment, and he ran a temperature. Dad was worried about him. I went up to Ernie's room to see if I could be of any help to him. Ernie thrust the letter toward me.
>
> "Read it," he said from the depths of his grief. "No. I'll tell you." Then he turned to the wall. He was physically sick for several days but he did not mention the letter again.
>
> Ag, Ernie told me, was not coming to America. She was going to marry an Italian major instead.
>
> In time Ernest felt better. He got out among his friends again....[Marcelline Hemingway, *At the Hemingways*, Boston, 1962, p. 188]

By the end of April Ernest had recovered sufficiently to jest about his situation in a letter to an old Red Cross buddy: "I am a free man! That includes them all up to and including Agnes. My Gawd man you didn't think I was going to marry and settle down did you?" (Baker, *Selected Letters*, p. 24). But before that he had written to another nurse from Italy, Elsie MacDonald, "telling her the news and adding that when Agnes disembarked in New York on her way home, he hoped that she would stumble on the dock and knock out all her front teeth" (Baker, *Ernest Hemingway*, p. 81).

In June he received another letter from Agnes, in which she told him that her Italian lieutenant's (his actual rank) aristocratic family had forbidden the marriage, so she would be coming home unmarried after all. Ernest did not answer this letter but wrote a buddy from the ambulance unit about it:

> Had a very sad letter from Ag from Rome yesterday. She has fallen out with her Major. She is in a hell of a way mentally and says I should feel revenged for what she did to me. Poor damned kid. I'm sorry as hell for her. But there's nothing I can do. I loved her once and then she gypped me. And I don't blame her. But I set out to cauterize out her memory and I burnt it out with a course of booze and other women and now it's gone. [Baker, *Selected Letters*, p. 25]

This diegesis we are constructing from various texts is not yet finished. It goes on for some time. After Ernest marries a woman about the same age as Agnes and moves to Paris, living mostly off her income, he writes a friendly letter to Agnes and receives a friendly reply in December of 1922:

> You know there has always been a little bitterness over the way our comradeship ended. . . . Anyhow I always knew that it would turn out right in the end, and that you would realize it was the best way, as I'm positive you must believe, now that you have Hadley. [Baker, *Ernest Hemingway*, p. 136]

A few months later he writes a sketch for a collection of vignettes that will be published in 1924 as *in our time*. Sometime before the final version is delivered to the Three Mountains Press in Paris (the date of composition is not known) he had begun a draft called "Personal." A pencil copy exists among the Hemingway papers. In Philip Young and Charles Mann's catalogue of the manuscripts it is described as beginning with the words "One hot evening in Milan they carried me up onto the roof" (*The Hemingway Manuscripts*, item 11C). For the published volume, this sketch was rewritten in the third person. It appeared as "chapter 10" in *in our time*, and it was virtually identical to what we know as "A Very Short Story," but the nurse is called "Ag" instead of Luz in this version, and the hospital is located in Milan instead of Padua. In short, this text gives us a diegesis closer to the one we can construct for Ernest Hemingway himself from the letters and other documents than does the later version. When the American publication of *In Our Time* was arranged, the little vignettes of the original *in our time* were used to separate the longer stories in the new volume and two of the original set were promoted to the status of stories. In this way the tenth vignette became "A Very Short Story," and Ag became Luz, Milan became Padua, and The Fair became a Loop department store. The changes were made, Hemingway said, to avoid possible libel suits: "Ag is libelous, short for Agnes," he wrote to Maxwell Perkins (discussing the 1938 publication of his collected stories—see Baker, *Selected Letters,* p. 469).

Brooding still over this episode, Hemingway began a novel called "Along With Youth," in which Nick Adams, the hero, was to be followed in his adventures as an ambulance driver "to a love affair with a nurse named Agnes" (Baker, *Ernest Hemingway,* p. 191). This manuscript stopped at page 27, with Nick still on a troop transport headed for Europe. But Hemingway continued to brood over this episode of his youth until he finally transformed Agnes into Catherine Barkley and laid her to rest in *A Farewell to Arms.*

Many texts, many diegeses. What can we say about them? First of all, it is clear that we are not dealing with an impersonal artist constructing aesthetic wholes, here, but with a dogged human being trying to produce texts that will pass as works, drawing upon one of the most painful events of his life for his material. As interpreters, what are we to make of the shift from Milan to Padua for the location of our diegesis, since nothing else is changed? Every Italian city has a duomo. The name Padua or Milan is there to generate with its apparent specificity "the effect of the real" as Roland Barthes calls it, though the precise city is not important. The fictional diegesis has a tidiness, of course, that actuality rarely assumes, and a sexuality that extends well beyond the events from which it derives. The need to add carnality to an affair that really was a "boy and girl" romance is especially notable now. Those words of Luz about the "boy and girl affair" are absurd when written by someone who had waited in bed while her crippled lover did her hospital work for her. As the words of Agnes von Kurowsky—which they may or may not actually be—they could be simply accurate.

We can also note that in life the Kid did not go back to the front;

she did, in effect, by volunteering to help with an epidemic. And he wrote hef at least as often as she wrote him. At one point five of his letters reached her in the same batch (Baker, *Ernest Hemingway*, p. 71). The gonorrhea, of course, which shocked Ernest's father so deeply that he mailed his copies of *in our time* back to the publisher, saying he "would not tolerate such filth in his house" (*At the Hemingways*, p. 219) was apparently an invention. About "friend or enema" we can only speculate.

The text produced by Hemingway responds to a double motivation. It wants to be art, to be a work that is complete in itself. But it also wants to rewrite life, to make its surrogate protagonist more triumphant as a lover, more active as a soldier, and more deeply victimized as a man than was the author himself.

Where does this leave the critic, the teacher, the student of literary texts? I hope it leaves them suspicious and flexible. I chose this Hemingway text for discussion because it *is* a very short story and it has interested me since I first read it as an undergraduate. I began to study it not knowing what I would find. I did the analysis first, then the scholarship. My work is not done. My own text is incomplete. So be it. My purpose, too, is perhaps unachieved, but lest it be misinterpreted as well, let me restate it here.

I do not wish to suggest that we jettison the critical ingenuity we have learned from the New Critics. Certaintly I will not give up my own. But I do wish to suggest that we approach fictions as texts traversed by codes rather than as formal artifacts. A semiotic approach, it seems to me, allows critic, teacher, student, and reader more scope for thought, more freedom and more responsibility, than a merely exegetical one. This Hemingway text is neither the greatest story ever told nor a horrible example. It is, in miniature, a model of all fictions—better than the man who made it, because he worked hard to make it that way, but still flawed, still a communication to be tested and weighed, not an icon to be worshiped. For all forms of idolatry, whether of gods, men, or literary works, teach us finally the worst of all lessons: to bend the knee and bow the head, when what we must do instead is examine everything before us freely and fearlessly, so as to produce with our own critical labor things better than ourselves.

8

UNCODING MAMA: THE FEMALE BODY AS TEXT

It is a tenet of semiotic studies—and one to which I fully sub-scribe—that much of what we take to be natural is in fact cultural. Part of the critical enterprise of this discipline is a continual pro-cess of defamiliarization: the exposing of conventions, the dis-covering of codes that have become so ingrained we do not notice them but believe ourselves to behold through their transparency the real itself. Nowhere is this process more important or more powerful than in our perceptions of our own bodies. We think we know ourselves directly, but both the "we" that know and the "selves" that are known are thoroughly permeated with signs: cul-turally coded to the core.

The study in this chapter might be subtitled "The Adventures of an Organ in Language and Literature." Before recounting these adventures, however, I must offer a warning and enter a dis-claimer, lest my enterprise be misconstrued. I am going to talk about body parts and body functions here, but not as one trained in anatomy and physiology might talk of them. Like all of us, I am an amateur of human sexuality, but my concern here is only indirectly with the realities of the matter. Certain signs of sexuality as they function in language, in psychoanalytic discourse, and in literature are the main objects of this study. I must admit, also, that much of what I have to say is not new but has been mentioned by feminist writers in one context or another already; though I believe the whole configuration has not yet been put together in quite the fol-lowing way, to which I have been led not as a feminist but as a semiotician.

We can begin by considering the Freudian myth of human socialization. I use the word "myth" advisedly, here, for several reasons. What Freud gives us is not a testable hypothesis so much as an intuitive narrative with explanatory power, resembling in this many other mythic structures of great cultural significance. In the Freudian mythos human infants pass through a sexual initiation ritual that enables them to join the social community, with their libidinal energies tamed by fear and envy, so that they can be civilized and discontented—like everybody else. This mythic process has several crucial moments, but perhaps the most crucial is the first sight—or, perhaps better, first noticing—of the genitals of a member of the opposite sex. In the Freudian mythos, the female infant sees the male penis, thus becoming aware of her own lack of that organ, and is left suffering from penis envy. The male infant, seeing the female body, also notices a lack, a deficiency, thus establishing in his mind the real possibility of losing his own organ. Henceforth, he walks in the shadow of the fear of castration.

There are other aspects of the Freudian scenario, of course—Oedipal feelings, displacements of desire, and so on—but for our purposes the crucial material is already before us. By a process of binary opposition, so characteristic of human thought—in both logic and mythology—male and female have been defined as a fullness and a deficiency, a presence and an absence, a plus and a minus, an "on" and an "off." The vagina and the penis, as an absence and a presence—the gap that needs filling and the magic wand that fills it—seem to divide the sexual world between them. And this is true not just of Freud but of the whole world of jokes, folktales, and fabliaux as well. There is one difficulty with this neat binary opposition, which does not trouble the bluff and hearty world of folk sexuality, but causes great trouble for Dr. Freud, who has studied anatomy and cannot easily overlook important body parts. Analyzing human sexuality and reconstructing it according to the perfect binary opposition of presence and absence, the good doctor—like a child putting together a clock he has taken apart "to see how it works"—discovers that he has a part left over. This part, which does not fit into the neat binary scheme, is what Freud called (in his essay on fetishism) "the real little penis of the woman, the clitoris." This masculine feature attached to the female body becomes a great burden for Freud. It mars the symmetry of absence and presence. He calls it "the normal prototype of an organ felt to be inferior" ("Fetishism," in *Sexuality and the Pyschology of Love*, p. 219). And he does everything he can to trivialize it, to criticize it, to erase it from the discourse of sex.

We shall return to this erasure later on, but first we should separate the sign from its referent a moment, to consider the curious fortunes of the word "clitoris" in language. In English, even its pronunciation remains unsettled. Most British dictionaries accent the second syllable; some American dictionaries put the accent on the first. The *Oxford English Dictionary*, that unequaled compendium of historical usage, places a double bar in front of the entry for this word, signifying "not naturalized in English." How appropriate, how natural, that this unnatural organ, this bit of "male" anatomy mysteriously attached to the female body, should not be naturalized in the language, either. Can this be a coincidence? We have no native slang word for it, either, that I have been able to locate—that is, no word like those old English words of few letters that are still carved, like runes, into schoolroom desks. We have an abbreviation of the signifier—"clit"—which I believe to be a recent formation; and I have found, in such an exotic place as the masturbatory letters James Joyce wrote to his common-law wife, Nora, several instances of the word "cockey"—a diminutive of the male term—that refer unambiguously to the clitoris. Aside from these formations, we seem to have no word in common parlance for this unnaturalized organ.

The dictionaries have still more to tell us. The *OED* gives us a definition: "a homologue of the male penis, present as a rudimentary organ in females of the higher vertebra." It is only an enthymemic hop, skip, and jump from here to the conclusion that every human female comes equipped with one, but the *OED* leaves its readers to draw that conclusion. The good gray dictionary also gives us the etymology of the word. The undomesticated English term has been imported directly from the Greek, *kleitoris*, which has the same meaning. Speculatively, the *OED* adds that the Greek word may "perhaps" be derived from the verb *klei-ein*, to shut. The unabridged Webster follows the *OED*, except that it confidently asserts that the Greek noun is derived from the verb that means "shut up." Thus is lexicological mythology established. A guess is introduced in one text under the protection of "perhaps."

In later texts the "perhaps" is forgotten; guesswork become knowledge.

The *Greek-English Lexicon* of Liddell and Scott (revised by Jones and McKenzie) will allow us to return to creative guesswork once again. The word κλειτορίς is both late and rare in Greek, appearing first in the second century A.D. in a medical text by one Rufus, called Περί Ονομασίας—"On Naming." Rufus has a verb, too, κλειτοριάξω, meaning "clitorize," to touch the clitoris. The Greek word κλειτορίς has also a second meaning, again a late formation, found in a discussion of rivers attributed to the Pseudo Plutarch. This secondary meaning is "jewel" or "gem." No modern dictionary has cared to see any connection between the two meanings, though similar metaphorical processes frequently connect the male genitalia and jewelry in popular speech and in literature.

In the *Lexicon* other words hover around this one. The adjective κλειτός means famous when applied to people, and splendid or excellent when applied to things. The verb κλείω meaning to shut or bar as in "bar the door" or "shoot the bolt," is indeed there, as the English language dictionaries suggest; but the noun κλείς is there as well, meaning bar, bolt, catch, hook, and in later Greek, "key." Yet all Webster has given us of this etymological richness is the laconic "shut up." Obviously, there is more to it than that. Most obviously, the noun "bar" or "key" rather than the verb "shut" seems the best candidate for the root of the word clitoris, through an obvious metaphoric process based on iconic similitude. The connection between the adjective "splendid" and the secondary meaning of κλειτορίς as "jewel" also seems obvious. Finally, the relation between the primary and secondary meanings of the Greek word κλειτορίς itself—the sexual organ versus the precious gem—is similar enough to other metaphoric linkages involving male organs that it should not surprise us. But how did all this get lost or mislaid? How did this whole paradigmatic structure evade the eyes of the lexicographers? We are dealing, I believe, with a widespread process of censorship—not a political conspiracy but a semiotic coding that operates to purge both texts and language of things that are unwelcome to the men who have had both texts and language in their keeping for so many centuries. This code is both unconscious in its operation and powerful in its action, for it derives its energy from a deeply felt male fear of feminine sexuality.

The male fear of feminine sexuality takes many forms. At its simplest and perhaps most benign, it is just the feeling that women experience a deeper, more thorough gratification from sex than men do. As a character in a story by Angela Carter ("A Souvenir of Japan," in *Fireworks* [New York, 1981], p. 8) puts it: "He told me that when he was in bed with me, he felt like a small boat upon a wide, stormy sea." The character who feels that way is a small-boned Japanese, making love to a large Anglo-Saxon woman, but I think many men, regardless of their skeletal and muscular structure, have felt similar things upon similar occasions. There is a male awe at full female sexual response, an awe which is often ready to turn nasty. This feeling is expressed in classic form by a remark actually made to a woman by her British lover during the quarrel that terminated their affair. Speaking of their lovemaking he said, "I would have enjoyed it more if you had enjoyed it less." One suspects that a significant portion of the whole male sex would endorse that proposition.

The suspicion that the female is sexier than the male appears in different forms in many human cultures. In the Third Book of Ovid's *Metamorphoses*, Jove, joking in a jovial mood with Juno, says, "Maior vestra profector est, quam quae contingit maribus voluptas." That is, "You women enjoy a greater pleasure in love than do your spouses." Ovid reports Juno's answer in direct discourse: "Illa negat" (she denied it). The dispute is settled by consulting Tiresias, who once accidentally turned himself into a woman and lived as one for seven years before conditions presented themselves that allowed him to resume his manly shape. The reply of Tiresias to the gods' question is presented by Ovid rather elliptically: "Iovis firmat" (He supported Jove). Whereupon Juno strikes the unfortunate arbiter blind and Jove compensates him with second sight—the ability to foresee the future.

We should notice a number of aspects of this story. First, given a choice, Tiresias has preferred to return to masculine form. Thus, his confirmation of Jupiter's view also trivializes sexuality. Yes, women have more pleasure, but men have more power. Tiresias knew what the phallus is all about—not pleasure but power. Ovid

was a good Roman, after all. And, like a good Roman, he also
played down the difference in the pleasure experienced by the two
sexes, as compared to the way this pleasure was described in his
Greek sources, one of which puts it this way:

> If the parts of love pleasure be counted as ten,
> Thrice three go to women, one only to men.
>> [Quoted in Vern L. Bullough, *Sexual Variance*, Chicago,
>> 1976, p. 114]

Similar myths exist in other cultures, most notably the Hindu myth
of Bhaṅgāsvana, as found in the *Mahābharata*. By means of a sex
change similar to that of Tiresias, King Bhaṅgāsvana begets a
hundred sons as a man and bears another hundred as a woman. The
God Indra then asks her if she wants to become a man again. She
says no: "The woman has in union with man always the greater
joy, that is why...I choose to be a woman" (Bullough, pp. 254–
55). Of course, the king originally wanted *sons* and incurred the
wrath of Indra by performing an impious rite to obtain them. And
only the sons are counted in the tale. If daughters are born, we do
not hear of them.

Sexual pleasure from India to Rome is opposed to power. The
men have power and the women have pleasure in all the versions of
this myth. But even this is not the whole story. The farther west the
myth moves, the more the pleasure itself is discounted. Bhaṅgāsvana rates it highly enough to remain a woman for its sake. Tiresias
does not. In Greece the woman's pleasure is ninefold greater than
the man's. In Rome, all we know is that Tiresias would not contradict the ruler of the heavens.

Is there a reality behind the myth? Do women have more pleasure? We cannot know and it does not matter. What matters is the
male fear that this is the case. It is some notion of the insatiable
sexuality of women that lies behind the talmudic prohibition
against a widow owning a male slave or even keeping a dog
(Abodah Zarah, 22b and Baba Meziah, 71a, as reported in Bullough, p. 79). There is a similar consideration operative in what is
called the "circumcision of women," a practice once widely
known in the Islamic world and still found, especially in North Af-
rica. "Circumcision" in these instances means primarily clitoridectomy. What we are really talking about here is female castra-

tion. This is the way Vern L. Bullough reports on this practice in *Sexual Variance:*

Male circumcision is carried out with a great deal of public ceremony, but female circumcision, where it exists, is usually done in private. It is not prescribed by the Koran, and where it is practiced, it is probably a pre-Islamic carryover. In some groups a needle and thread is stuck through the top of a young girl's clitoris, which is then pulled down and cut off as far as it protrudes. In other groups only the exposed tip is cut off. In some societies, particularly in southern Egypt and the Sudan, it has been customary to do more drastic circumcisions and to cut off the labia minora and, at times, even the labia majora. In Egypt, under the late Gamal Abdel Nasser, there was considerable discussion over the abolition of female circumcision, since it had been condemned by a United Nations Committee as a torture and laceration to girls. The Sudan also has been interested in abolishing the practice and has passed some legislation to that effect.

In Muslim countries one of the contradictions inherent in female circumcision, an operation that excises the clitoris, is that the Muslims believe and teach that the clitoris is the source and wellspring of all female passion. This implies that clitoral excision is a more or less deliberate attempt to make women less sensuous and is, therefore, contrary to the Koran. One Sudanese who justified the practice claimed that the

circumcision of women releases them from their bondage to sex, and enables them to fulfill their real destiny, as mothers. The clitoris is the basis for female masturbation; such masturbation is common in a hot climate; the spiritual basis of masturbation is fantasy; in fantasy a woman broods on sexual images; such brooding inevitably leads a woman to spiritual infidelity, since she commits adultery in her heart, and this is the first step to physical infidelity, which is the breaker of homes.

Apparently, partial excision of the clitoris does not entirely remove sexual feeling, but it does leave the woman much slower to respond, requiring her to take a great deal of time to reach orgasm. This has often led women to encourage their husbands to use hashish and other intoxicants to slow down their performance. Radical excision, as practiced in some parts of the Islamic world (as well as elsewhere), leaves women with virtually, no ability to reach orgasm. [219–20]

In introducing some evidence about clitoridectomy, I do not wish to single out Islamic or African culture as unique. For one thing, we can, if we look, find Victorian doctors in England practicing this operation on unruly women and reporting that it has a wonderfully calming effect upon them. But more important, this ritual, whether sanctified by custom or justified as clinical practice, is in fact an acting out of male fears and wishes that are widely distributed, if not universal. In Western Europe, from the Enlightenment on, this process has been primarily a semiotic one, not enacted on the suffering bodies of actual women but inscribed in printed texts. Still, the texts have created their share of suffering—as texts frequently do. I propose, now, to look at three well-known texts that deal with female sexuality, focusing specifically on the fortunes of the clitoris in these works. My texts are John Cleland's pornographic novel of 1749, *The Memoires of Fanny Hill;* Sigmund Freud's *Three Essays on Sexuality* (German edition 1905, first English translation 1910, final revised edition 1924, final English edition 1953); and D. H. Lawrence's *Lady Chatterley's Lover* (The "Author's Popular Edition" of 1929).

John Cleland virtually introduced the pornographic novel into English literature in 1749, with *Fanny Hill*, which is still quite popular and is especially useful for our purposes since it is so clearly an example of male projection. Cleland gives us sex, not as it was or is, but as the men of his time wished it to be. Fanny is a literary descendant of Defoe's Moll Flanders and a remote ancestor of our own Xaviera Hollander. She is the happiest of hookers, reporting her experiences in elegant figurative language, in which a spade is never called a spade. Sex is described early and often, in loving detail, but always in accordance with a curious code that not only limits what is reported but also controls what can be seen and prescribes what can occur. For our purposes, the main features of the code are these:

1. There is no way a woman can achieve sexual satisfaction except by insertion of the male "machine" in the female "gap."
2. Pleasure for the female is directly proportional to the size of the male "machine."
3. Unless the male is inadequate (which rarely occurs in this world) this pleasure always occurs simultaneously in both sexes and is marked by a simultaneous emission of fluid in both.

4. The number of times a woman achieves satisfaction is always
   equal to the number of times the male does, except when the
   male is inadequate. The woman is never satisfied more times
   than the man.
5. The male genitals are described in considerable detail and are
   individualized by unique features as often as possible.
6. The female genitals are described in a kind of soft focus, as if
   airbrushed, so that no details beyond hair color are reported.
   The clitoris is certainly invisible and for all practical purposes
   nonexistent.

There are other rules governing the erotic code of *Fanny Hill*,
including a frequent linking of pleasure and pain for women, a total
exemption from venereal infection for all characters, and a prevailing insistence that all's well that ends well—but for our purposes
the six rules above are the most important. The disappearance of
the clitoris (Rule 6) is really a corollary of the first rule, the master
rule, one might say, of the entire book. A woman cannot achieve
full satisfaction alone; nor can two women together achieve it, for
only the male organ can appease the desire of an aroused woman:

> I laid me down on the bed, stretched myself out ...requiring any
> means to divert or allay the rekindled rage and tumult of my desires,
> which all pointed strongly to their pole: man. I felt about the bed as if I
> sought for something that I grasped in my waking dream, and not
> finding it, could have cried for vexation; every part of me glowing
> with simulated fires. At length I resorted to the only present remedy,
> that of vain attempts at digitation, where the smallness of the theatre
> did not yet afford room enough for action. [Cleland, *Fanny Hill*, Sig-
> net edition, pp. 43–44]

This passage comes soon after another in which the virginal Fanny
does achieve a kind of climax by "digitation" (the only such experience in the book); thus the second passage serves as a corrective to the first, establishing Rule 1, the necessity of the male "machine" for full satisfaction of the female, beyond all doubt. Even
when the innocent Fanny is used by her bedmate Phoebe to obtain
some sexual pleasure, it is done by Phoebe using Fanny's hand as if
it were the missing male organ. "Digitation" is always a vain pur-
suit in *Fanny Hill* because the busy fingers can never find a suitable

object, the author having removed it or, as we shall see, relocated it.

In the perhaps two dozen descriptions of the female body on display, in a variety of poses calculated to make visible as much as can be seen of the female genitalia, no trace of the clitoris can be discerned. But this organ is not entirely absent from the book. It is mentioned on one occasion and only one—not called by its name, of course, since no sexual organ is referred to literally in this most figurative of texts, but neither is it given the lavishly honorific treatment regularly accorded the "animated ivory" of the male member: it is simply a "soft fleshy excresence" (p. 99). Even on this singular occasion the clitoris is not actually visible but is found by a young man exploring with his fingers what Fanny herself calls "the secrets of that dark and delicious deep" (p. 99). By a slight anatomical adjustment, Cleland has put the clitoris where it ought to be in the sort of world he has constructed, inside what Fanny calls "that soft pleasure-conduit pipe" (p. 100). Cleland has given us in this book an erotic utopia, a pornotopia, where all is arranged to suit the male reader, down to the smallest details.

So much for the pornotopic dream of the Age of Reason. Such arrangements are not possible for the clinical psychoanalyst. Sigmund Freud, who, as a medical doctor, knew anatomy very well, dealt with this unruly organ in yet another way. Being too civilized to amputate it and too scientific to relocate it, he simply ordered it to cease and desist. The crucial passage is in his *Three Essays on the Theory of Sexuality* (New York, 1975, pp. 86–87):

LEADING ZONES IN MEN AND WOMEN. Apart from this I have only the following to add. The leading erotogenic zone in female children is located at the clitoris, and is thus homologous to the masculine genital zone of the glans penis. All my experience concerning masturbation in little girls has related to the clitoris and not to the regions of the external genitalia that are important in later sexual functioning. I am even doubtful whether a female child can be led by the influence of seduction to anything other than clitoridal masturbation. If such a thing occurs, it is quite exceptional. The spontaneous discharges of sexual excitement which occur so often precisely in little girls are expressed in spasms of the clitoris. Frequent erections of that organ make it possible for girls to form a correct judgement, even without any instruction, of the sexual manifestations of the other sex:

they merely transfer on to boys the sensations derived from their own sexual processes.

If we are to understand how a little girl turns into a woman, we must follow the further vicissitudes of this excitability of the clitoris. Puberty, which brings about so great an accession of libido in boys, is marked in girls by a fresh wave of *repression*, in which it is precisely clitoridal sexuality that is affected. What is thus overtaken by repression is a piece of masculine sexuality. The intensification of the brake upon sexuality brought about by pubertal repression in women serves as a stimulus to the libido in men and causes an increase of its activity. Along with this heightening of libido there is also an increase of sexual overvaluation which only emerges in full force in relation to a woman who holds herself back and who denies her sexuality. When at last the sexual act is permitted and the clitoris itself becomes excited, it still retains a function: the task, namely, of transmitting the excitation to the adjacent female sexual parts, just as—to use a simile—pine shavings can be kindled in order to set a log of harder wood on fire. Before this transference can be effected, a certain interval of time must often elapse, during which the young woman is anaesthetic. This anaesthesia may become permanent if the clitoridal zone refuses to abandon its excitability, an event for which the way is prepared precisely by an extensive activity of that zone in childhood. Anaesthesia in women, as is well known, is often only apparent and local. They are anaesthetic at the vaginal orifice but are by no means incapable of excitement originating in the clitoris or even in other zones. Alongside these erotogenic determinants of anaesthesia must also be set the psychical determinants, which equally arise from repression.

When erotogenic susceptibility to stimulation has been successfully transferred by a woman from the clitoris to the vaginal orifice, it implies that she has adopted a new leading zone for the purposes of her later sexual activity. A man, on the other hand, retains his leading zone unchanged from childhood. The fact that women change their leading erotogenic zone in this way, together with the wave of repression at puberty, which, as it were, puts aside their childish masculinity, are the chief determinants of the greater proneness of women to neurosis and especially to hysteria. These determinants, therefore, are intimately related to the essence of femininity.

We know, now, that Freud was wrong about this. His "normal" woman whose clitoris abandons its excitability is a myth. If she exists, it is because he has created her, even as he created countless others who wanted to be that woman but could not make their bodies fit his code. In reading the passage critically, what must strike us as most incongruous is Freud's apologetic lapse into the figurative discourse of the pornographer right in the middle of it. His pine shavings kindling the harder wood remind us of the language of Cleland before him, or perhaps of the discourse now employed in manuals for newlyweds sponsored by religious organizations, directing innocent young couples toward the solaces of lawful delights. Freud himself has become the prisoner of his own binary code. The woman is absence; the man is presence; and that awkward "little penis of the woman," as he called it, must go:

> For unto every one that hath shall be given, and he shall have abundance: but from her that hath not shall be taken away even that which she hath. And cast ye the unprofitable servant into outer darkness: there shall be weeping and gnashing of teeth. [Matthew 25: 29–30, adapted]

D. H. Lawrence, of course, comes to liberate us from our sexual inhibitions. He tells us so himself, in the preface he wrote for his unabridged "Popular" edition of *Lady Chatterley's Lover:*

> And this is the real point of this book. I want men and women to be able to *think* sex, fully, completely, honestly and cleanly. Even if we can't *act* sexually to our complete satisfaction, let us at least think sexually, complete and clear. All this talk of young girls and virginity, like a blank white sheet on which nothing is written, is pure nonsense. A young girl and a young boy is a tormented tangle, a seething confusion of sexual feelings and sexual thoughts which only the years will disentangle. Years of honest thoughts of sex, and years of struggling action in sex will bring us at last where we want to get, to our real and accomplished chastity, our completeness, when our sexual act and our sexual thought are in harmony, and the one does not interfere with the other. [p. v]

An ambitious program. How close does Lawrence come to achieving it? Two crucial passages will provide most of the answer. The first is one of the most famous in the book. In it the gamekeeper, Mellors, is playing doctor with Connie Chatterley—quite literally—giving her a lecture on her own anatomy in his charming northern dialect:

"Tha's got such a nice tail on thee," he said, in the throaty caressive dialect. "That's got the nicest arse of anybody. It's the nicest, nicest woman's arse as is! An' ivry bit of it is woman, woman sure as nuts. Tha'rt not one o' them button-arsed lasses as should be lads, are ter! Tha's got a real soft sloping bottom on thee, as a man loves in 'is guts. It's a bottom as could hold the world up, it is."

All the while he spoke he exquisitely stroked the rounded tail, till it seemed as if a slippery sort of fire came from it into his hands. And his finger-tips touched the two secret openings to her body, time after time, with a soft little brush of fire.

"An' if tha shits an' if tha pisses, I'm glad. I don't want a woman as couldna shit nor piss."

Connie could not help a sudden snirt of astonished laughter, but he went on unmoved.

"Tha'rt real, tha art! Tha'rt real, even a bit of a bitch. Here tha shits an' here tha pisses: an' I lay my hand on 'em both an' like thee for it. I like thee for it. Tha's got a proper, woman's arse, proud of itself. It's none ashamed of itself, this isna." [p. 263]

Two aspects of this passage should be noted. First, Connie's femininity is defined against an opposed masculinity. Her "tail" is beautiful because it is not like a "lad's." Second, and most important, something is missing from the anatomy lecture. The pornotopic airbrush that removes blemishes from the photographs of beauty queens has touched this scene as well, eliminating that organ that has too much of the "lad" in it to belong on a "proper woman's arse."

Gone, but not forgotten, the unruly organ turns up in a passage less well known than the love scene we have just been considering. Here is Mellors telling Connie about his former wife's sexual behavior:

But she treated me with insolence. And she got so's she'd never have me when I wanted her: never. Always put me off, brutal as you like. And then when she'd put me right off, and I didn't want her, she'd come all lovey-dovey, and get me. And I always went. But when I had her, she'd never come-off when I did. Never! She'd just wait. If I kept back for half an hour, she'd keep back longer. And when I'd come and really finished, then she'd start on her own account, and I had to stop inside her till she brought herself off, wriggling and shouting, she'd clutch clutch with herself down there, an'then she'd come off, fair in ecstasy. And then she'd say: That was lovely! Gradually I got sick of it: and she got worse. She sort of got harder and harder to bring off, and she'd sort of tear at me down there, as if it was a beak tearing at me. By God, you think a woman's soft down there, like a fig. But I tell you the old rampers have beaks between their legs, and they tear at you with it till you're sick. Self! Self! Self! all self! tearing and shouting! They talk about men's selfishness, but I doubt if it can ever touch a woman's blind beakishness, once she's gone that way. Like an old trull! And she couldn't help it. I told her about it. I told her how I hated it. And she'd even try. She'd try to lie still and let *me* work the business. She'd try. But it was no good. She got no feeling off it, from my working. She had to work the thing herself, grind her own coffee. And it came back on her like a raving necessity, she had to let herself go, and tear, tear, tear, as if she had no sensation in her except in the top of her beak, the very outside top tip, that rubbed and tore. That's how old whores used to be, so men used to say. It was a low kind of self-will in her, a raving sort of self-will like in a woman who drinks. Well in the end I couldn't stand it. We slept apart. [pp. 242–43]

It is as if Lawrence is simply fleshing out with dramatic interaction the bare bones of a Freudian scenario. The supposed masculinity of Mrs. Mellors is what makes her so terrible—a masculinity expressed in her desire to take charge, to be in control of the sexual scene, but concentrated physically in her clitoral orientation, presented metaphorically as a predatory beak. It is just such an orientation that Connie herself has given up, in moving from her earlier, unsatisfactory lover to Mellors. Exactly as Freud does, so Lawrence, too, orders the clitoris to cease and desist, orders women to be more "feminine," to become the perfect binary opposites that men require, and to become less sexual in the process.

Freud is an intertext behind Lawrence, but that is only a minor part of the point of this study. The major point is that Freud's and Lawrence's texts are governed by the same masculine code, shaped by a fear of feminine sexuality expressed as a need to define woman as lacking what the male possesses and as perpetually deficient without the presence of the male. The same message that some cultures have inscribed directly on the female body is embodied in the Freudian and Lawrentian texts, and from these comes the inscription of this message upon many other minds and texts. It would be nice to think that by laying bare the workings of this code we have uncoded the female body and can now perceive its truth—and perhaps Masters and Johnson, Shere Hite, and others have brought us closer to some kinds of truth about the body at last. In the original dance of the seven veils, one comes at last to a direct perception of reality, with no veil, no code, between us and what we see. Semiotic studies must caution us on this point. The veils are not removed but displaced by others that seem transparent only for a time. We may feel like saying of the organ whose vicissitudes we have been following, "It is meet that we should make merry and be glad: for this thy sister was dead and is alive again, and was lost, and is found" (Luke 15:32); but we would perhaps do better to wonder what we have lost or hidden by this very finding.

GLOSSARY OF SEMIOTIC TERMINOLOGY

*Nous entrons ici dans les embarras (et les disgrâces) de la ter-
minologie.*

G. Genette

Code Semioticians hold that all intelligibility depends upon
codes. Whenever we "make sense" of an event it is because we
possess a system of thought, a code, that enables us to do so. Light-
ning was once understood as the gesture of a powerful being who
lived in the mountains or the sky. Now we understand it as an elec-
trical phenomenon. A mythic code has been displaced by a scientific one. Human languages are the most developed instances of
coding that we know, but codes exist that are sublinguistic (facial
expression, for instance) and supralinguistic (literary conventions,
for instance). Interpretation of complex human utterances involves the appropriate use of a number of codes simultaneously.

Connotation Meanings attached loosely to a word by its history
of use are called connotations. In the semiology of Roland Barthes
connotations are evoked rhetorically, and all manipulative or
"classic" texts seek to limit and control the "metonymic skid" of
connotation by systematizing or closing the connotative flow. The
writer of fiction "creates character" by limiting the number of attributes associated with a particular proper name.

Denotation Usually understood as a proper or literal meaning,
sometimes including the notion of designation or reference (q.v.),
denotation is naming. Its extreme form is the "proper" name with a
single referent, but we also denote classes of objects with terms
like "cat" and "tree." In the semiology of Roland Barthes and his
followers, denotation has come to be associated with closure of
meaning, and hence with censorship and political repression. In

143

extreme reaction against the oppressive literalness of denotation, Barthes has abolished it, asserting that there are no such things as denotations, that these are only connotations, and that we call the last one, the connotation we rest upon, "denotation." This often seems hyperbolical but it is a useful corrective to the belief that "literal" meanings are natural laws or divine commandments.

Diegesis (diegetic)   Both diegesis and mimesis are aspects of the representation of actions or events. Put most simply, what is shown or enacted is mimetic; what is told or reported is diegetic. In the strictest sense, a diegesis is a sequence of actions or events construed by an interpreter from a narrative text.

Discourse   This word is used in a number of related but far from identical ways. It can refer to the words or text of a narrative as opposed to the story or diegesis. It can also refer more precisely to those aspects of a text which are appraisive, evaluative, persuasive, or rhetorical, as opposed to those which simply name, locate, and recount. We also speak of "forms of discourse" as generic models for utterances of particular sorts. Both the sonnet and the medical prescription can be regarded as forms of discourse that are bound by rules which cover not only their verbal procedures but their social production and exchange as well.

Icon (iconic, iconicity)   In Peirce's theory of signs any given sign is iconic to the extent that it signifies by virtue of some resemblance or similitude between the sign and what it stands for. Pictures and diagrams are the most common iconic signs, but the sound of the word "woof" is to some degree iconic of a dog's bark. All onomatopoetic effects depend upon aural iconicity.

Index (indexical)   In Peirce's theory of signs a sign is indexical to the extent that there is a phenomenal or existential connection between the sign and what it signifies. Friday's footprint in the sand in *Robinson Crusoe* is taken by Crusoe as an index of the presence of men. Involuntary facial and bodily gestures are taken to be indices of emotional states and therefor truer than mere verbal reports on them (symbols). A blush, a faint, a trembling of the limbs once spoke powerfully. But as codes are understood, the involuntary and unconscious come more fully under control. Blushes can be consciously created. The index yields to the conventional symbol.

Interpretant In Peirce's theory of signs, every sign that is understood gives rise to another sign in the mind of the interpreter. This second sign is the interpretant of the first. For instance, you might show me a picture of a banana, causing the word for banana (in my language) to come to my mind as an interpretant. Or, you might show me the word and a picture or icon might come to my mind. We frequently interpret icons with symbols and symbols with icons. This notion of one sign being interpreted by another has been taken up by Eco and Derrida and presented as an infinite regress called unlimited semiosis.

Intertext (intertextual) For semioticians like Barthes, Genette, Kristeva, and Riffaterre this word has very special meanings, which vary from one to the other. The common principle is that, just as signs refer to other signs rather than directly to things, texts refer to other texts. The artist writes and paints, not from nature but from his or her predecessors' ways of textualizing nature. Thus, an intertext is a text lurking inside another, shaping meanings, whether the author is conscious of this or not. Balzac's *Eugénie Grandet* is an intertext for Barthelme's "Eugénie Grandet," of course, but this laying bare of intertextuality is a parody of the process, which is usually less obvious and more complex in its operations. Parallel to the unlimited semiosis of signs we have the infinite regress of texts as well. All elegies are intertexts for W. S. Merwin's "Elegy."

Mimesis (mimetic) Holding its traditional sense of imitation or representation, this term is now used in two more specific senses. Opposed to diegesis, it means enactment of what is represented as opposed to imagination of the events based on a verbal text. The reader of a play engages in a diegetic activity; the actor of a play speaks the words and mimes the actions of the text. This is mimesis. In another context, mimesis is opposed to semiosis. Here, mimesis is the attempt to take language as literally representational. When this is impossible—as in metaphor, metonymy and other figures of speech—the interpreter must move from mimesis to semiosis. That is, the reader must give up trying to move from words to things and must accept the principle of unlimited semiosis, moving from word to word, sign to sign. (See INTER-PRETANT.)

Paradigm (paradigmatic) From Saussure semioticians have taken the notion that every sign exists in its code as part of a paradigm, a system of relationships that connect it to other signs by resemblance and difference, before the sign appears in an utterance. In language, a word is paradigmatically related to synonyms, antonyms, other words with the same roots, words that sound like it, and so on. This paradigmatic structure offers the potential field for substitutions that result in metaphors, puns, metonyms and other figures. The notion of paradigm, if pushed far enough, yields unlimited semiosis. (See SYNTAGM.)

Pragmatics Part of a triad used by Charles Morris and others to define the concerns of semiotic study, pragmatics refers to those aspects of communication that are functions of the situation in which an utterance is made: especially to the relationship between speaker and listener. Such things as acoustic difficulty (distance, noise) are a part of pragmatics, but so are emotional relationships and power relationships. Irony is often grounded in pragmatics. (See also SEMANTICS and SYNTACTICS.)

Reference (referent) In Peirce's semiotic theory every sign has an object to which it refers, but the object need not have a physical existence. It may be a thought, a dream figure, or an imaginary creature like a unicorn. In the tradition of empirical or positive semantics only statements that have actual referents are taken seriously, because only they may have truth value. An extreme position in this tradition is that words derive their meanings from the things to which they refer. The Saussurean view on this matter is that words take their meanings from their paradigmatic structure: their relationship to other words in language, so that reference is arbitrary or accidental, and in any case outside the province of semiotics. The extreme of this position is that there is no such thing as reference. In Peirce's semiotic, icons and indices are defined by their relation to their referents, symbols by their place in a conventional or arbitrary system. Thus Peirce allows a flexibility that is denied by both the extreme empiricists and the extreme semioticians. I follow Peirce in this matter.

Semantics (semantic)   In the semiotics of Charles Morris, semantics refers to that aspect of semiotics that deals with the meanings of signs before their use in a particular utterance. (The other aspects are syntactics and pragmatics—q.v.) The semantics of Morris leads to a study of what Saussure called associations and later semioticians call paradigms (q.v.). Paul Ricoeur has tried to argue that semiotics is concerned only with paradigmatic relationships and that semantics is the study of propositions and their referential meaning. In ordinary discourse the word has a debased meaning: "merely semantic," meaning without reference or consequence.

Semiology (semiologist)   Parisian semioticians have retained Saussure's term (sémiologie) for their field; hence it remains a useful way of distinguishing their work from the international semiotics now current in Eastern Europe, Italy, and the United States.

Semiosis   As used by Riffaterre this word is opposed to mimesis (q.v.). In reading a poem or understanding any verbal figure the interpreter finds that a "literal" or mimetic reading is frustrated and a "figurative" meaning must be generated. The process of generating a figurative meaning is semiosis. It involves a return to the paradigmatic structure surrounding individual words and to the intertextual structure surrounding a given poetic text.

Sign   For Saussure a sign is a double entity, consisting of a signifier (a sound-image) and a signified (a concept). For Peirce a sign is something that stands for something else to somebody in some respect or capacity. The Peircean sign has an *object* to which it refers, an *interpretant* which it generates in the mind of its interpreter, and a *ground* upon which the interpretation is based. Different grounds lead to three types of sign: icon, index, and symbol (q.v.). The followers of Saussure have modified the notions of a signifier and signified (q.v.).

Signified   In Saussure this is the concept, which, linked to a particular sound-image, constitutes a sign. But the notion of "concept" has proved too fixed, too mentalistic, for later semiologists like Roland Barthes. The term "signified" is still useful as a way of talking about a sign's meaning without raising the question of reference, but in other ways it has lost much of its usefulness (See SIGNIFIER.)

Signifier The acoustic image that, linked to a concept, constitutes a sign in Saussurean linguistics. Later semiologists, following Barthes and Lacan have rejected the notion of any fixed connection between signifier and signified, arguing that signifiers "float," attracting signifieds which merge with them to become signifiers for still other signifieds. The general result of this has been to debase the word signified and to create confusion, as witnessed by the inconsistent translations of *signifiant* and *signifié* in *S/Z*. It is safe to say that neither term has any precise meaning at present—which perhaps justifies the semiological position on the matter.

Story As opposed to *discourse,* story refers to the events and situations evoked by a narrative text. As opposed to *plot* (in the theories of the Russian formalists and others) it refers to the events in their chronological order, despite any rearrangements in the plotting. A combination of these two meanings equates story with *diegesis* (q.v.). In current semiotic theory the story or diegesis is always a production of the reader of a text, based on the signs in the text but never totally controlled by them.

Symbol In Peirce's terminology this word has a precise meaning, referring to that type of sign which signifies by virtue of an arbitrary, conventional habit of usage. The Saussurean sign, in which signifier and signified are connected by convention only, in an arbitrary or "unmotivated" manner, is equivalent to the Peirceian symbol. It is important that these two founders of semiotic study agree on this crucial matter. It is also important that Peirce goes on to name two sign-functions (iconic and indexical) that are not arbitrary or conventional, while Saussure's followers simply extend Saussure's notion of the linguistic sign or word to all signs, verbal and nonverbal. In the space opened up by this difference, much of the internal debate within semiotic studies now takes place. The word "symbol" is widely used with varying meanings, of course, and must always be interpreted with care.

Syntagam (syntagmatic)   In post-Saussurian linguistics this word is opposed to paradigm (paradigmatic). Paradigm refers to a word's connection with other words in language as a whole outside of any particular utterance. Syntagm refers to a word's relation to other words (or a grammatical unit's relation to other units) within a particular speech act or utterance. Meaning is obviously a matter of both syntagmatic and paradigmatic functions. Because speech always expresses itself as a flow of verbal signs in time, syntagmatic functions are sometimes called linear. By a further metaphoric stretch, syntagm becomes horizontal and paradigm vertical. (See PARADIGM.)

Syntactics   Related to syntax, and hence to syntagm, syntactics is the part of semiotics (in Charles Morris's definition) that is concerned with the rules which govern utterance and interpretation. In this sense, it means something very much like grammar. It is to be distinguished from pragmatics, the study of conditions that surround utterance, in particular the relationship between speaker and audience and the general situation of the discourse. (See PRAGMATICS and SEMANTICS.)

Text   A set of signals transmitted through some medium from a sender to a receiver in a particular code or set of codes. The receiver of such a set of signals, perceiving them as a text, proceeds to interpret them according to the code or codes that are available and appropriate. To approach a literary utterance as a text is to consider it, in this manner, as open to interpretation though related to certain generic norms. In this sense *text* is opposed to *work,* which implies a closed and self-sufficient entity. This is not a rigid distinction but a matter of emphasis and nuance.

SELECT BIBLIOGRAPHY

This bibliography is limited in a number of specific ways. It is bounded fundamentally by my belief that, truly, "less is more" in bibliography; long lists are impressive but often not very helpful. It is also restricted to book-length texts in the English language (except for Jakobson's indispensable essay on linguistics and poetics). I have elected, in most cases, not to repeat titles mentioned in my earlier book on structuralism, and I have included no works that I cannot recommend with more than half a heart.

BACKGROUNDS TO SEMIOTICS

A little linguistics is a dangerous thing. Still, one must risk it. Saussure's *Course in General Linguistics* (New York: McGraw-Hill, 1966) supplemented by Benveniste's *Problems in General Linguistics* (Coral Gables: University of Miami, 1971) constitute the way to begin. C. S. Peirce's theory of signs should be encountered in his own formulations. The most accessible version is chapter 7 of Justus Buchler's *Philosophical Writings of Peirce* (New York: Dover, 1955). Freud, too, is a major part of the background to semiotics. From the bewildering array of his texts the most important for semiotics are chapter 6 of *The Interpretation of Dreams* ("The Dream-Work") and two studies that emphasize language: *The Psychopathology of Everyday Life* and *Jokes and Their Relation to the Unconscious*. These are all available currently in popular editions.

HANDBOOKS, GUIDEBOOKS, CRITIQUES, AND SURVEYS

Bailey, R. W.; Matejka, L.; and Steiner, P., eds. *The Sign: Semiotics Around the World.* Ann Arbor: Michigan Slavic Publications, 1978. This is a collection of essays on different topics by different writers. Like all such collections it is uneven. But it includes a substantial number of helpful studies of individuals and national "schools" of semiotics. Among these are T. Todorov on St. Augustine, E. Bruss on Peirce & Jakobson, W. Steiner on American semiotics (especially Charles Morris), N. Bruss on psychoanalysis, L. Kritzman on Greimas, J. Féral on Kristeva, and J. Fanto on speech act theory.

151

Barthes, Roland. *Elements of Semiology*. New York: Hill and Wang, 1967. This is not an elementary book but a book that discusses fundamental aspects of semiotics in a subtle and original way. Most accessible are Barthes's discussions of "the garment system, the food system, the car system, the furniture system." His treatment of the sign is important as a revision of Saussure that pushes semiotics even further away from a concern with representation, reducing Saussure's "psychologistic" notion of "concept" to a less specific entity, the "something" that is meant by the user of the sign.

Culler, Jonathan. *Structuralist Poetics*. Ithaca: Cornell University Press, 1975. This is the fullest and subtlest introduction to structuralist literary theory and criticism. Both its summaries and critiques of writers such as Jakobson and Greimas are excellent.

Eco, Umberto. *A Theory of Semiotics*. Bloomington: Indiana University Press, 1976. This represents almost ten years of thinking through and rethinking the basic problems of semiotics. It is closely reasoned and richly illustrated: a fundamental treatment of the nature of codes and the processes of sign production.

Hawkes, Terence. *Structuralism and Semiotics*. Berkeley: University of California Press, 1977. This book takes full advantage of earlier studies of structuralism to offer the clearest and most succinct introduction to literary semiotics that we have.

Lemaire, Anika. *Jacques Lacan*. Boston: Routledge & Kegan Paul, 1977. In this book (first published in Belgium in 1970) Lemaire not only presents the ideas of Lacan and his school, she also explicates for us the relationship between structuralism and psychoanalysis. For this reason her guidebook to Lacanian thought is an important introductory text for students of semiotics.

Sturrock, John. *Structuralism and Since*. New York: Oxford University Press, 1979. This is a fine little book, with excellent discussions of Lévi-Strauss by Dan Sperber, Barthes by Sturrock, Foucault by Hayden White, Lacan by Malcolm Bowie, and Derrida by Jonathan Culler.

Vološinov, Valentin. *Freudianism: A Marxist Critique*. New York: Academic Press, 1976 and *Marxism and the Philosophy of Language*. New York: Seminar Press, 1973. A member of the circle of Mikhail Bakhtin, Vološinov published the first of these two books in 1927 and the second in 1929. Together with Bakhtin's work, these two books laid the foundations for later eastern European semiotics. Even today, they are readable, provocative works in these well-edited editions. The second book has been rightly called a prolegomenon for Soviet semiotics.

ESSAYS IN LITERARY SEMIOTICS

Barthes, Roland. *Image-Music-Text.* New York: Hill Wang, 1977. This collection of essays selected and translated by Stephen Heath includes the very important "Rhetoric of Image," "Introduction to the Structural Analysis of Narratives," and "From Work to Text."
——. *S/Z.* New York: Hill and Wang, 1974. This is still the fullest, richest, and most successful application of semiotic methods to the analysis of a single fictional text that we have. The translation contains a number of errors, including at least eight places where the French *signifié* (signified) is translated as signifier (*signifiant*). Let the reader beware.

Bassoff, Bruce. *Toward "Loving": The Poetics of the Novel and the Practice of Henry Green.* Columbia: University of South Carolina Press, 1975. Insufficiently recognized, this is a pioneering and largely successful attempt to apply semiotic concepts to the analysis of an English novel.

Chatman, Seymour. *Story and Discourse.* Ithaca: Cornell University Press, 1978. A clear and direct exposition and illustration of the basic concepts of the semiotic analysis of narrative structures as developed by Barthes, Todorov, and especially Genette.

Derrida, Jacques. *Writing and Difference.* Chicago: The University of Chicago Press, 1978. For students of literary semiotics the most crucial essays in this collection are the two critiques of structuralism (one, ten), the two discussions of Antonin Artaud (six, eight), and the consideration of "Freud and the Scene of Writing" (seven).

Eco, Umberto. *The Role of the Reader.* Bloomington: Indiana University Press, 1979. A collection of essays written over twenty years, this book includes some excellent discussions of semiotic theory in the opening chapters, a very useful fable about esthetic language in the Garden of Eden, and, for English-speaking readers, two analyses of "closed" works (*Superman* and the James Bond novels of Ian Fleming) that are accessible, entertaining, and good examples of semiotic analysis.

Foucault, Michel. *Language, Counter-Memory, Practice.* Ithaca: Cornell University Press, 1977. These essays and interviews were selected by Donald Bouchard. The essays are all oriented toward language, and a number of them deal with literature as well. Especially important are "Language to Infinity," "The Father's 'No'," and "What is an Author."

Genette, Gérard. *Narrative Discourse.* Ithaca: Cornell University Press, 1980. This excellent translation by Jane Lewin of Genette's "Discours du récit" from *Figures III* is one of the two or three most important works of semiotic analysis of fiction currently available in English. Drawing his examples from Proust's *Recherche,* Genette develops a rigorous model for the analysis of time and point of view in narrative structures.

Jakobson, Roman. "Linguistics and Poetics" (in Sebeok, ed. *Style in Language.* Cambridge: M.I.T. Press, 1960, pp. 350–77). This truly seminal essay can also be found in the deGeorge anthology, *The Structuralists* (New York: Doubleday Anchor Books, 1972). This is the place where much later work in the semiotics of literary discourse begins.

Kermode, Frank. *The Genesis of Secrecy.* Cambridge: Harvard University Press, 1979. Working mainly with the Gospel of Mark, Kermode delicately and patiently elaborates the main points of difference between hermeneutic and semiotic interpretation. He is too civilized to say bluntly that this is his intention (or even to allow the word "semiotics" to sully his pen), but this is what he does, in full awareness of the related work of Barthes and Genette.

Kristeva, Julia. *Desire in Language.* New York: Columbia University Press, 1980. This collection of essays from *Polylogue* and Σημειωτιχη᾽ represents the work of ten years and constitutes, in the words of the subtitle "a semiotic approach to literature and art." The essays grow increasingly complex, difficult, and important as one proceeds through the book, moving from dutiful discussions of Bakhtin and Barthes to more daring and original speculations on the nature of signification in verbal and visual texts.

Lotman, Yuri. *Analysis of the Poetic Text.* Ann Arbor: Ardis, 1976. This is a major work by a major writer on literary theory. In it, Lotman first presents a theory of poetry and then applies it to a dozen Russian poems (with English translations). This is a clear, direct, and thoughtful book.

———. *Semiotics of the Cinema.* Ann Arbor: University of Michigan, 1976. Slight, and perhaps undernuanced, this is a sound introduction to the elements of film and film analysis.

———. *The Structure of the Artistic Text.* Ann Arbor: University of Michigan, 1977. This is a major statement by the leading critic in the Soviet group of semioticians known as the Tartu school. In it are formulated the general principles that receive more specific application in the two works mentioned above.

Mukarovsky, Jan. *Structure, Sign, and Function.* New Haven: Yale University Press, 1978. As a theoretician and critic, Mukarovsky belongs to the Prague circle of structuralists, along with Roman Jakobson. In the development of eastern European semiotics, he mediates between the early formalists, the Bakhtin group, and the present Tartu school. This collection of nonliterary essays includes the important "Art as a Semiotic Fact," "Time in Film," and "On the Current State of the Theory of the Theatre."

————. *The Word and Verbal Art*. New Haven: Yale University Press, 1977. The predecessor to the above volume, this one includes the author's essays on literature.

Pratt, Mary Louise. *Toward a Speech Act Theory of Literary Discourse*. Bloomington: Indiana University Press, 1977. As its title proclaims, this approach owes more to the speech-act philosophy of Austin, Grice, and Searle than to structuralism. In fact, it begins with a critique of Prague school structuralism. But its emphasis on the literary "speech situation" and discourse analysis make it interesting for American students of semiotics.

Riffaterre, Michael. *Semiotics of Poetry*. Bloomington: Indiana University Press, 1978. This book develops a theory of poetic composition and interpretation, using examples drawn mainly from French poetry of the past two centuries, according to the most extreme and rigorous assumptions of Parisian *sémiologie*. The argument and the interpretations are brilliant in conception and execution. Though many will find its antireferential position unpalatable, all serious students of poetry should read this book.

Smith, Barbara Herrnstein. *Poetic Closure*. Chicago: University of Chicago Press. 1968. Though she has never claimed to be a structuralist or semiotician and has indeed been a persistent critic of those who do, much of her practice in this book is compatible with eastern European semiotics if not with Parisian *sémiologie*. The book as its subtitle makes clear, looks at the semantic and syntactic devices used to achieve or imply the completion of poetic discourse.

————. *On the Margins of Discourse*. Chicago: University of Chicago Press, 1978. More theoretical and more sophisticated than its predecessor, this book works in the territory at present disputed by speech-act philosophers, structuralists and other theorists of discourse and its interpretation. Her views have a strong affinity with those of such eastern European semioticians as Bakhtin and Vološinov. Her concern here is more with the theory of language, literature, and communication, than with specific acts of interpretation.

Todorov, Tzvetan. *The Poetics of Prose*. Ithaca: Cornell University Press, 1977. This is a formidable collection of critical essays, ranging from detective fiction and the Arabian Nights to Henry James and Antonin Artaud in subject matter. The essays are lucid, logical, and usually turn on a point of structure or a formal figure. Together with Genette's *Narrative Discourse* and Barthes's *S/Z*, this is one of the major texts in the semiotic study of fiction.

INDEX